Anyone Can DRAW HORSES!

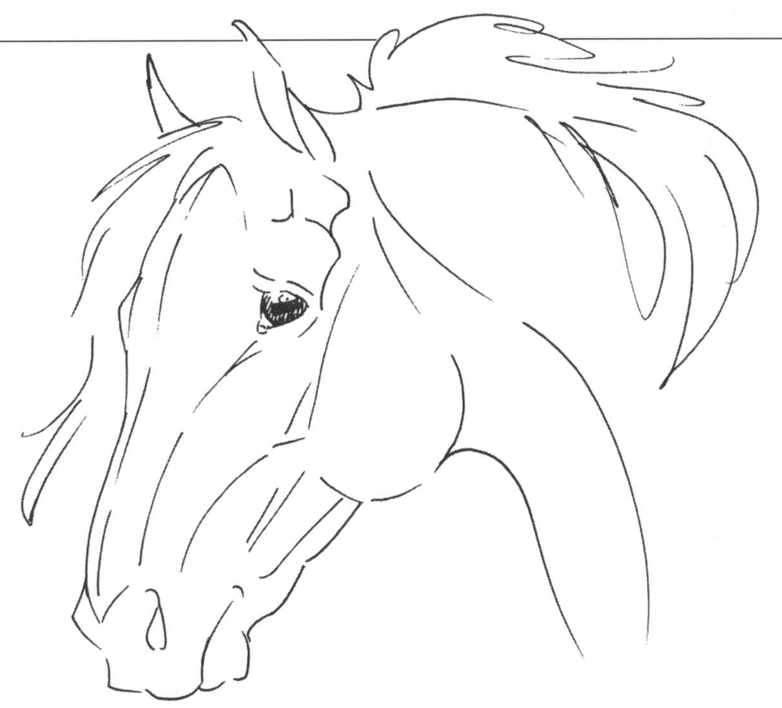

By June V. Evers

Published by Horse Hollow Press, Inc.

This book is dedicated to the late Sam Savitt, whose artwork and friendship inspired me throughout my life.

Published by Horse Hollow Press, Inc., PO Box 456, Goshen, NY 10924, Phone: 800-414-6773.
www.horsehollowpress.com.

Thank you to Blake Banta and Curvon Horse Clothing, the makers of the legendary and fabulous Baker™ Blankets. Ask for Baker™ Blankets, sheets, fly covers, and anti-sweat sheets at your local tack store. www.bakerblankets.com

As always, an extra special thank you to Jim Kersbergen.

MADE COMPLETELY IN THE U.S.A.
1st Printing 2003
09 10 11 12 — 10 9 8 7

ISBN: 0-9638814-6-9

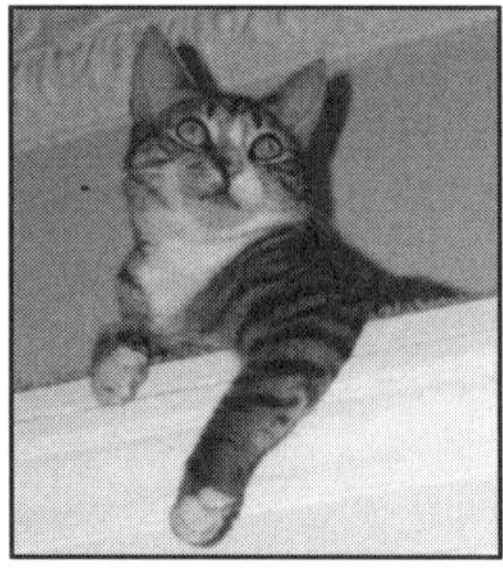

Office Manager

Table of Contents

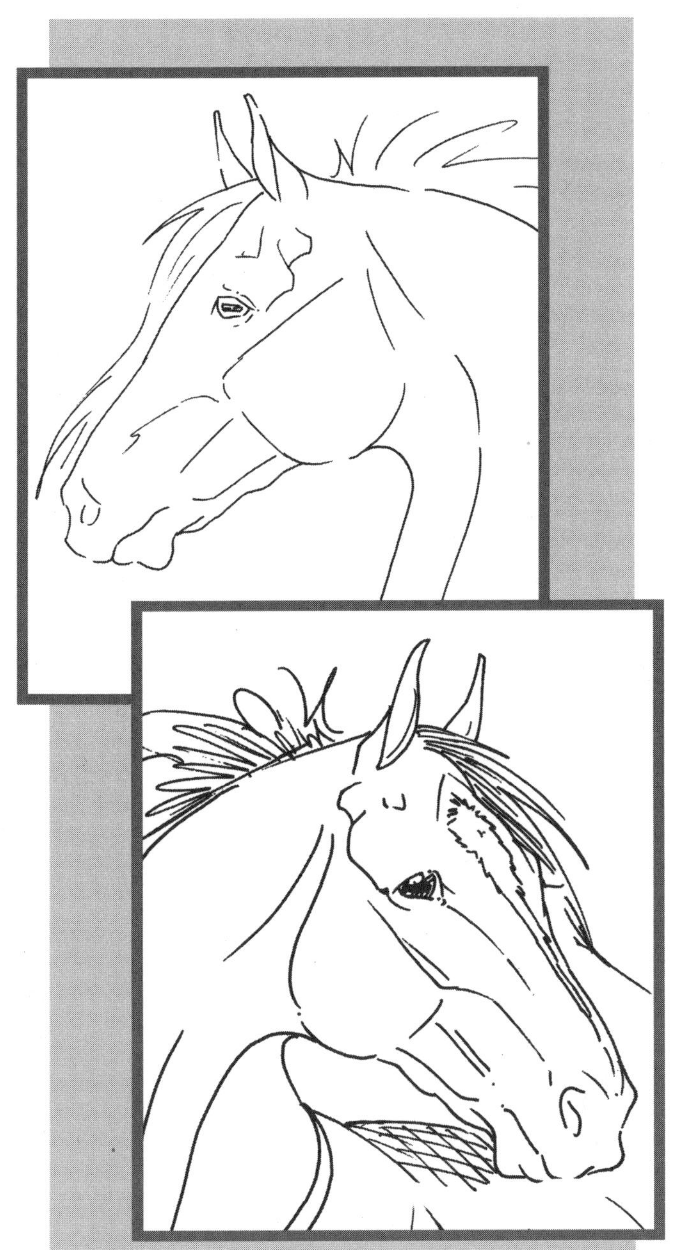

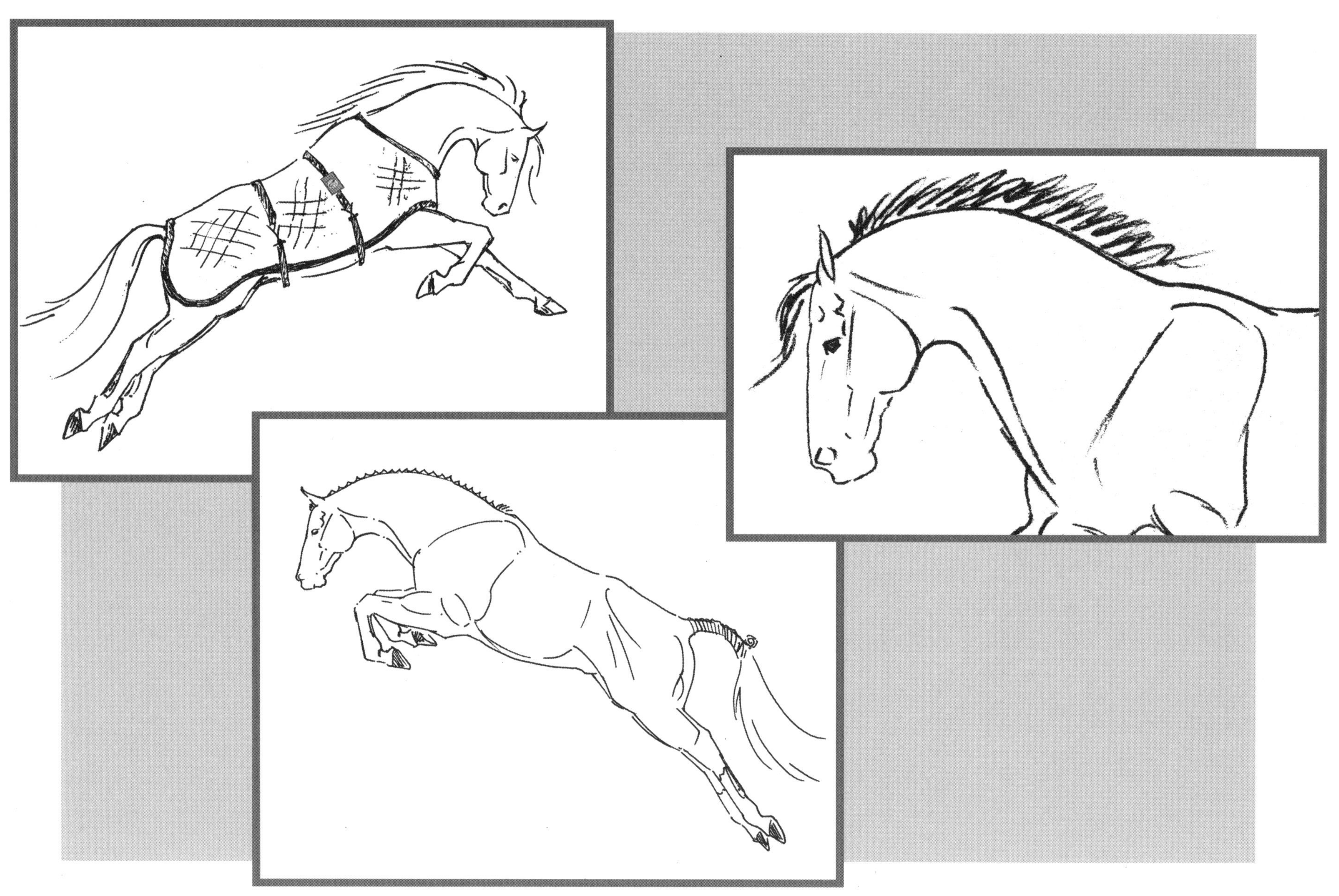

Introduction

Before You Begin

1. I work best in a fineline marker or an old-fashioned pencil, the kind you'd have in grade school. (I guess it's from years of doodling while I was in school or at work—much to the chagrin of my many teachers and bosses.) Start with a pencil. There are several pencil weights available; 2B, 4B, 6B. And as you progress, experiment with different mediums (drawing tools). Try everything!

2. Any paper will do. I work on marker layout paper which is very much like copy machine paper or school notepaper. Again, it's probably from years of working on paper that was on hand while I worked at a job or during school. As you become more experienced, you can try papers with an ultra-smooth finish or something with a little tooth. Tooth means there is a roughness to the paper.

3. Your work area is important, too! It goes hand-in-hand with the *actual* time that you *can* work. Either set up a specific place in your home designated for your work or, since we are all busy, place paper and pencil by the computer, in front of the TV, or near the phone. Practice anytime you're doing something *mindless*.

Some notes

1. Sketching and taking the time to really look at a real horse is always the best. Bring a sketchpad wherever you go.

2. However, doodling is the best way to practice. While doodling, you're not putting undue pressure on yourself to create a masterpiece. And sometimes those doodled images become pure magic — a masterpiece!

3. Throughout this book, you'll find exercises that include tracing horses. While you might think tracing is cheating, it is not. It is a wonderful way to teach your mind and your drawing hand and get the feel for the correct distances between knee and ankle, withers and croup, etc.

4. Check out the work of other artists past and present. Refer to their work whenever you are stuck drawing a particular part of the horse that's difficult. Seeing how other artists have done it is a great help. Look up Sam Savitt, Paul Brown, Sir Alfred Munnings, and Edgar Degas.

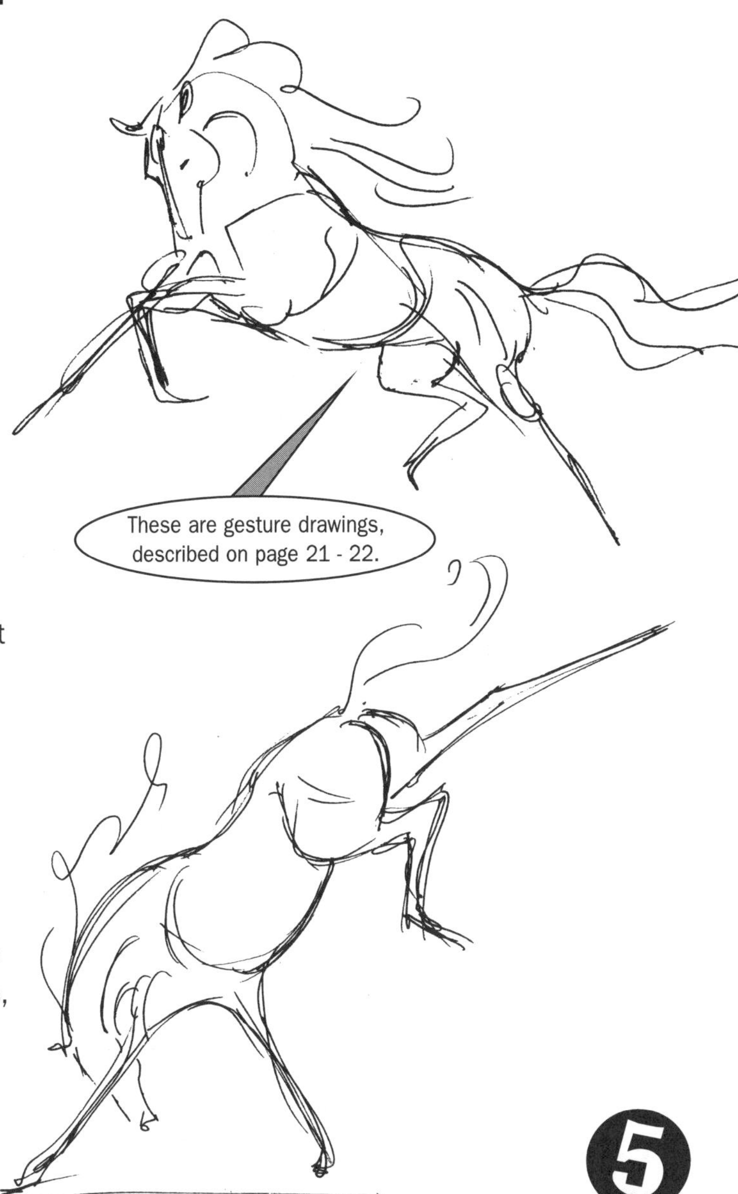

Getting Started

Before we begin, let me briefly introduce four different techniques I use to start drawing. I'll explain each technique in detail in the following sections. Try all these methods to find what works best for you.

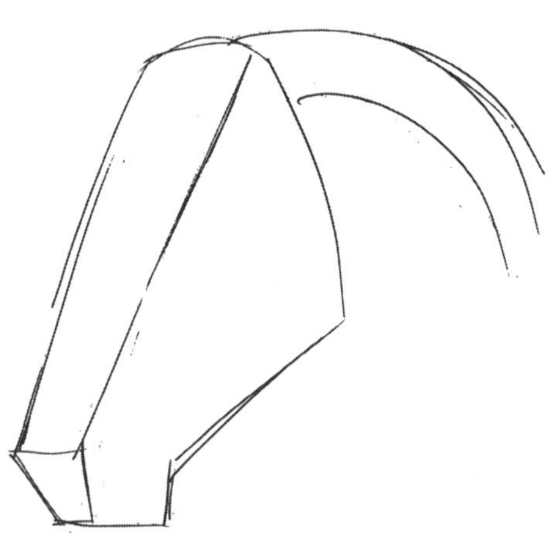

1 Geometric

Here, I start with a boxy shape to get the basic structure of the horse head or body. Then I refine the drawing around that box to create my horse.

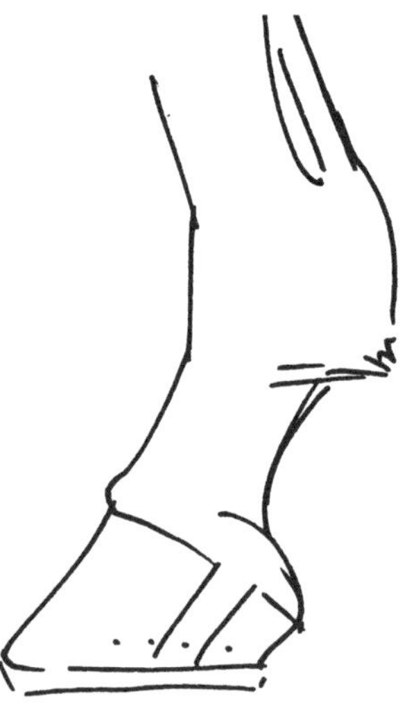

2 Line-by-line

This is actually the most difficult. You must innately learn where every line, bump and bulge needs to go and transfer that down onto paper. Tracing real horses in photos or drawings will really teach you the feel of how long or short each part of the horse is.

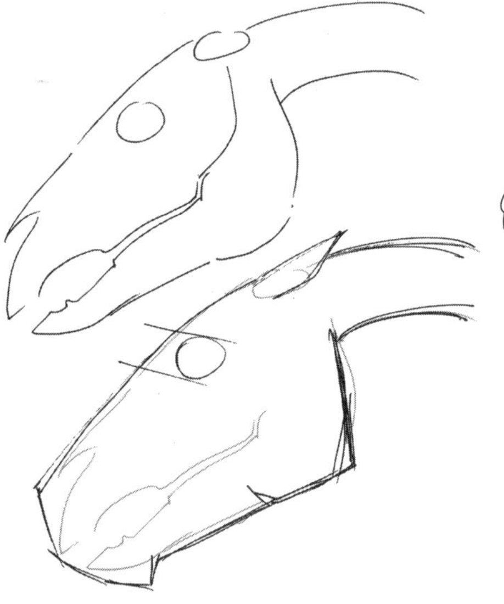

3 Anatomy

This technique is great for drawing horses showing emotion. When you're drawing a horse's head showing fear or anger, knowing exactly where to put the jaws and teeth when they're bared makes your drawing more credible.

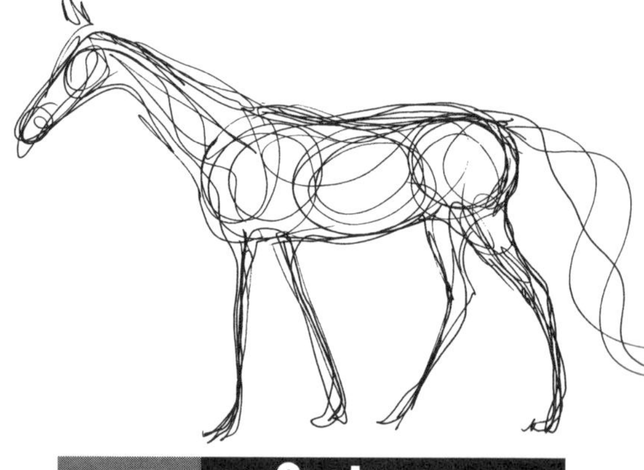

4 Gestures

This is the most energetic way to start a drawing. A gesture drawing is really just a bunch of squiggles that help you loosen up your arm and get the energy you feel about the horse down on paper. This energy conveys movement in your drawing. You can really anchor a leg onto the ground or make that bucking horse *really* buck. This technique works best when you're drawing a horse in motion.

DRAWING THE

Horse's Head

in 6 easy steps!

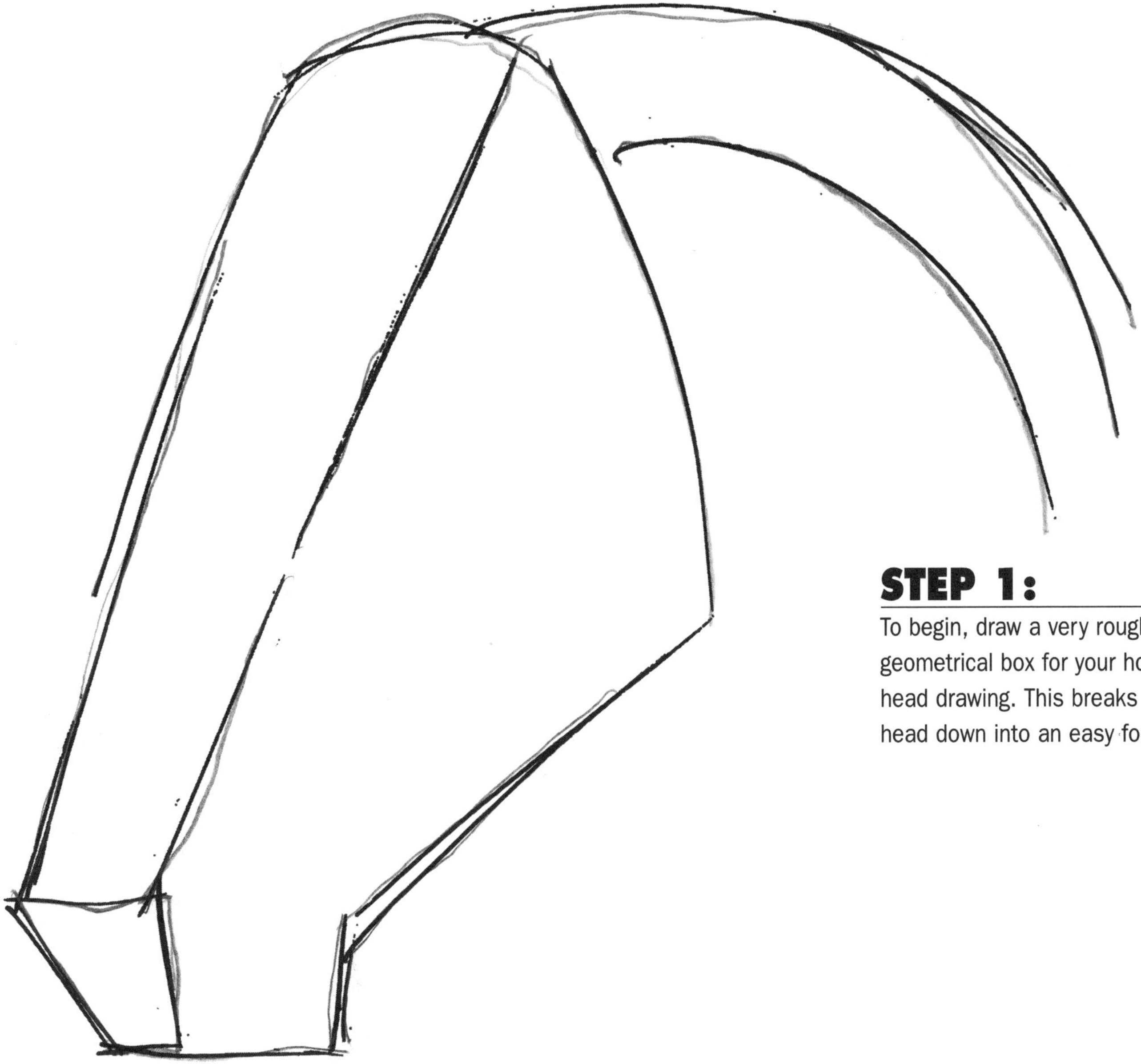

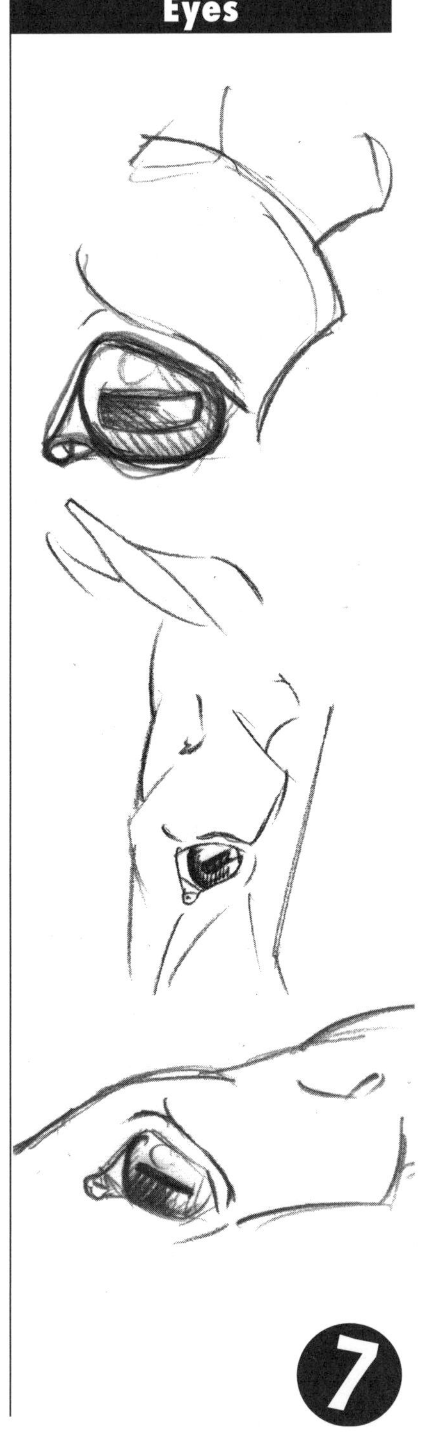

STEP 1:

To begin, draw a very rough geometrical box for your horse's head drawing. This breaks the head down into an easy form.

Head shape

Arabian

Thoroughbred

Draft

STEP 2:

Then start to add a contour line (a simple, confidently drawn line, not sketchy) for the facial features.

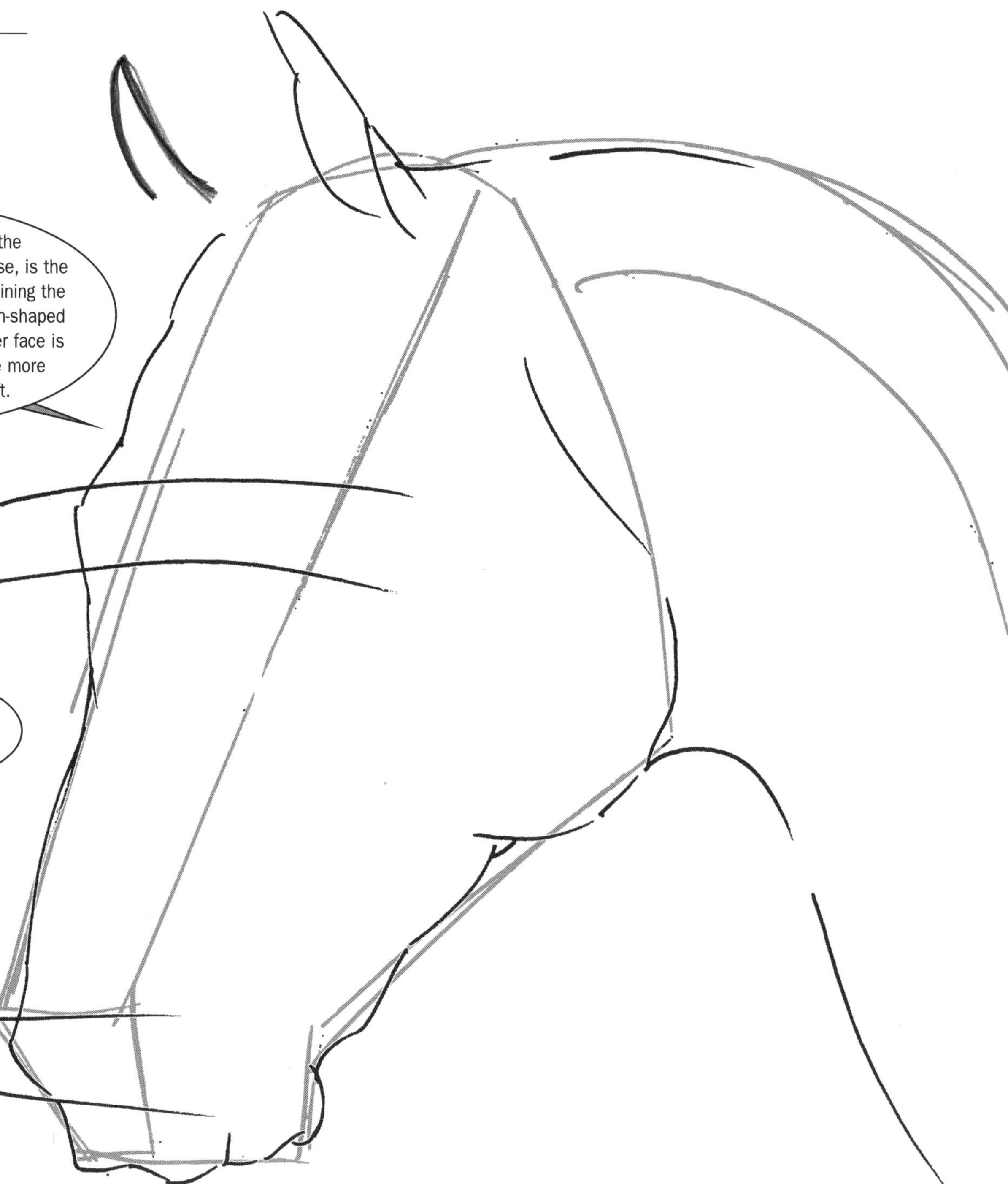

STEP 3:

Add the eyes and nostrils and a few lines to delineate facial structure.

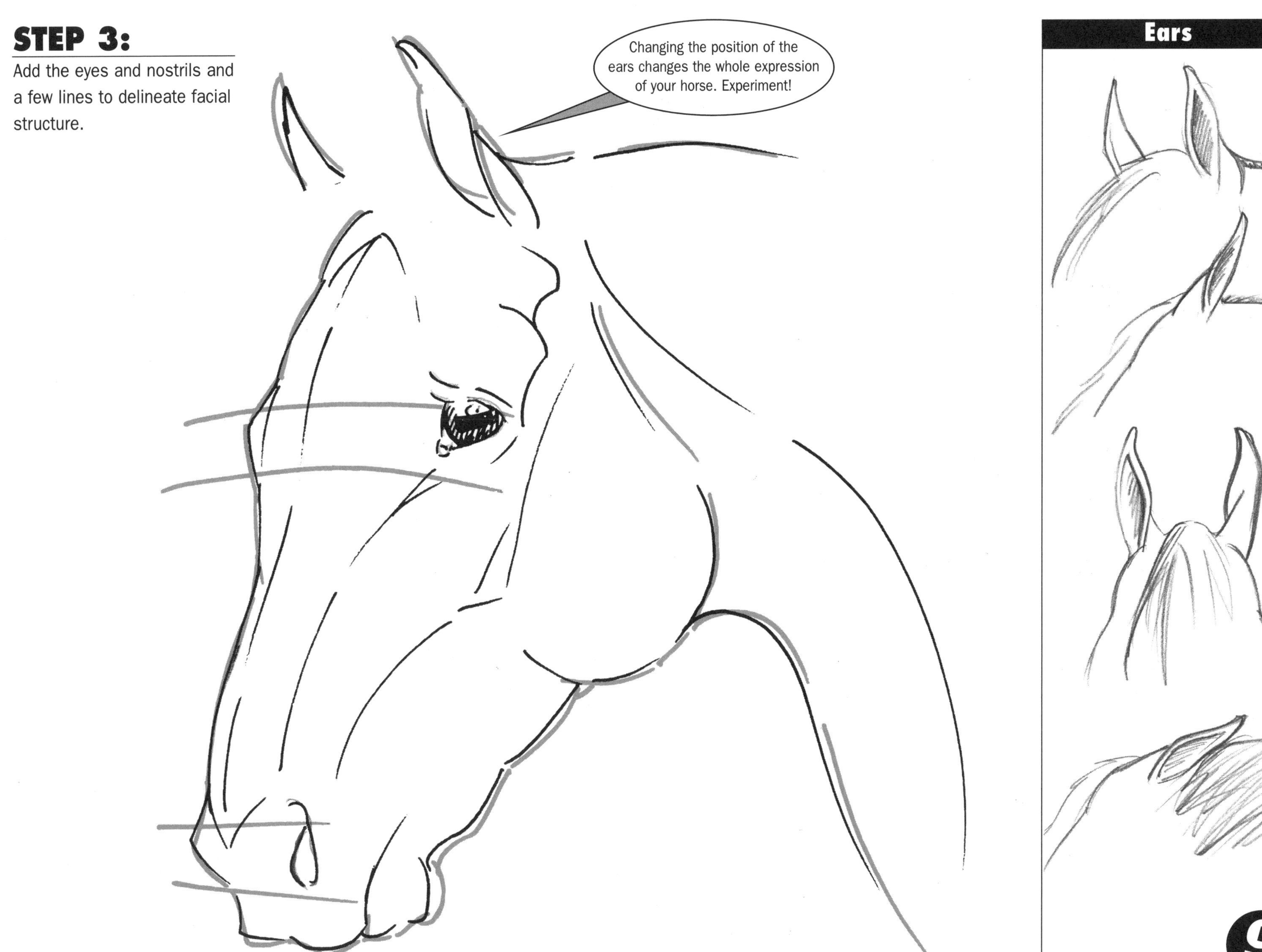

Ears

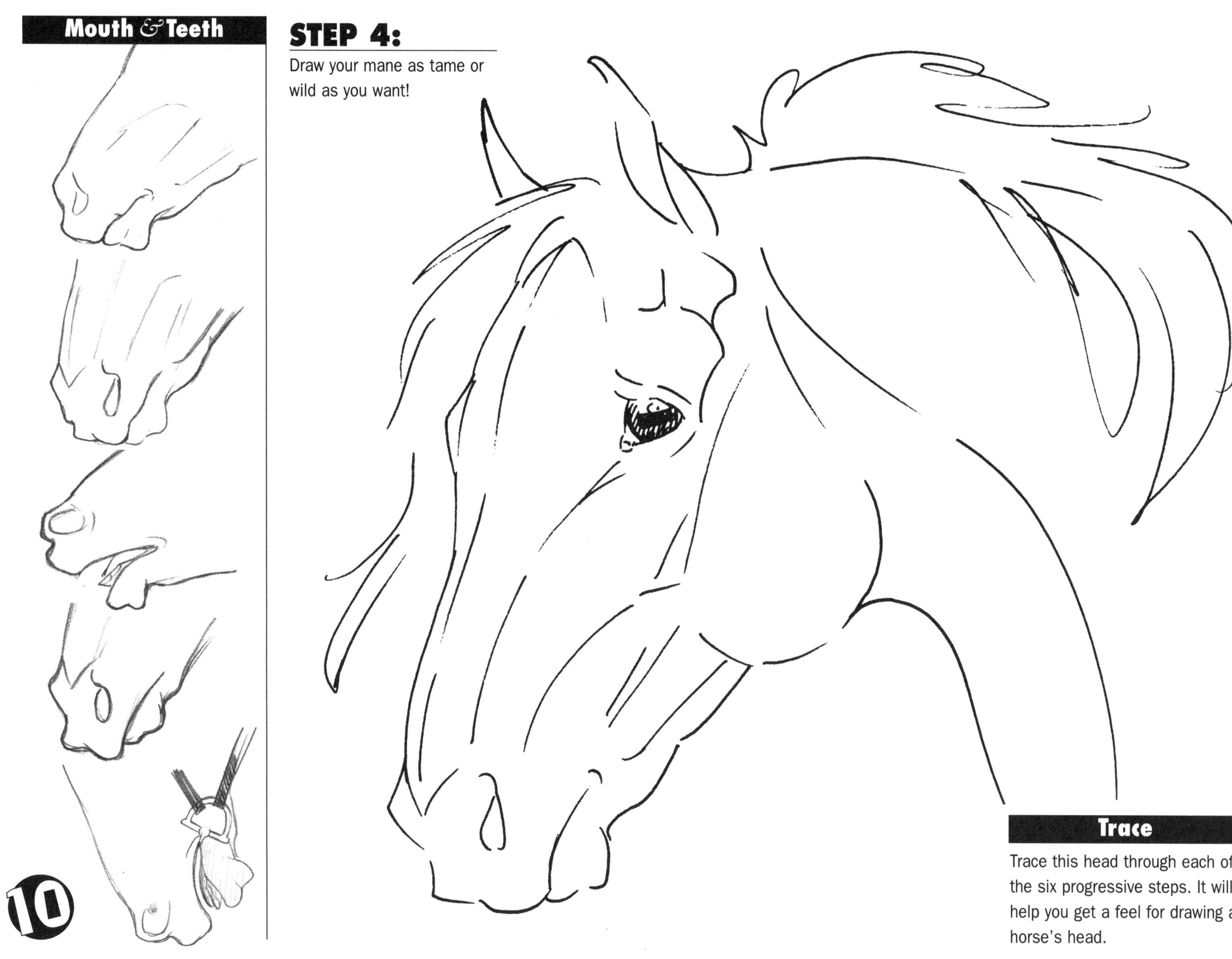

Mouth & Teeth

STEP 4:

Draw your mane as tame or wild as you want!

Trace

Trace this head through each of the six progressive steps. It will help you get a feel for drawing a horse's head.

STEP 5:

Add the shading! With a pencil, very loosely cross-hatch following the structure of the horse.

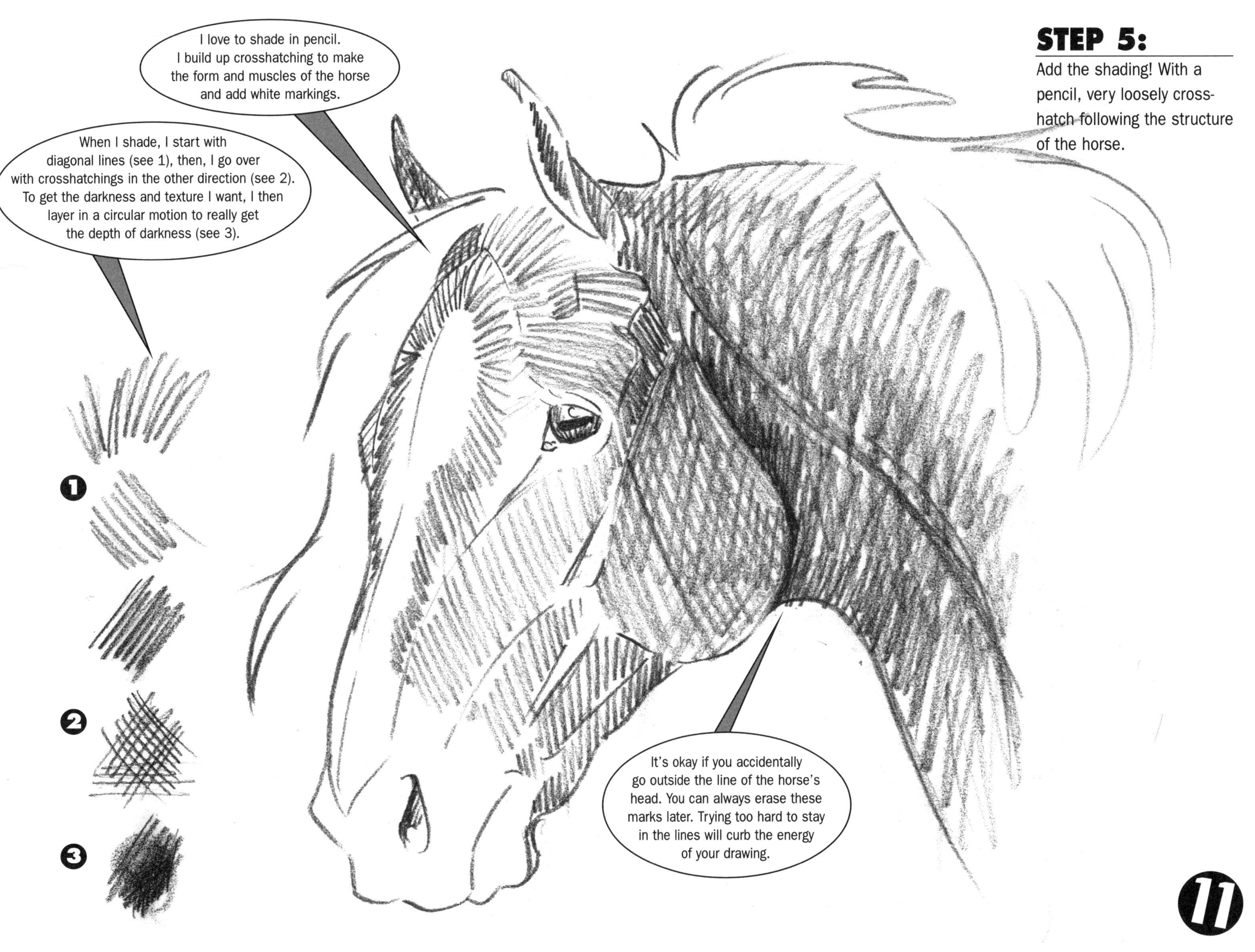

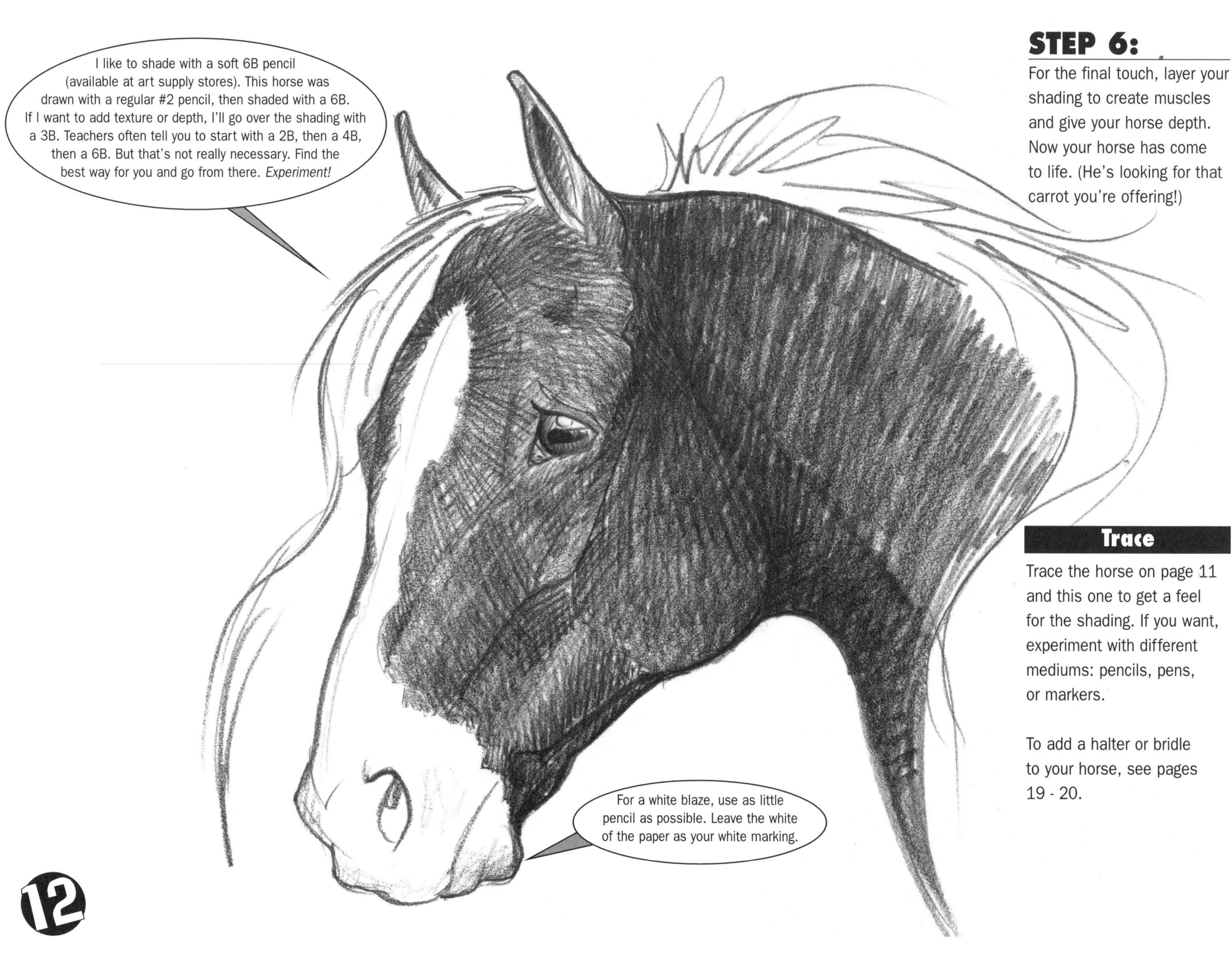

STEP 6:

For the final touch, layer your shading to create muscles and give your horse depth. Now your horse has come to life. (He's looking for that carrot you're offering!)

Trace

Trace the horse on page 11 and this one to get a feel for the shading. If you want, experiment with different mediums: pencils, pens, or markers.

To add a halter or bridle to your horse, see pages 19 - 20.

Trace this horse!

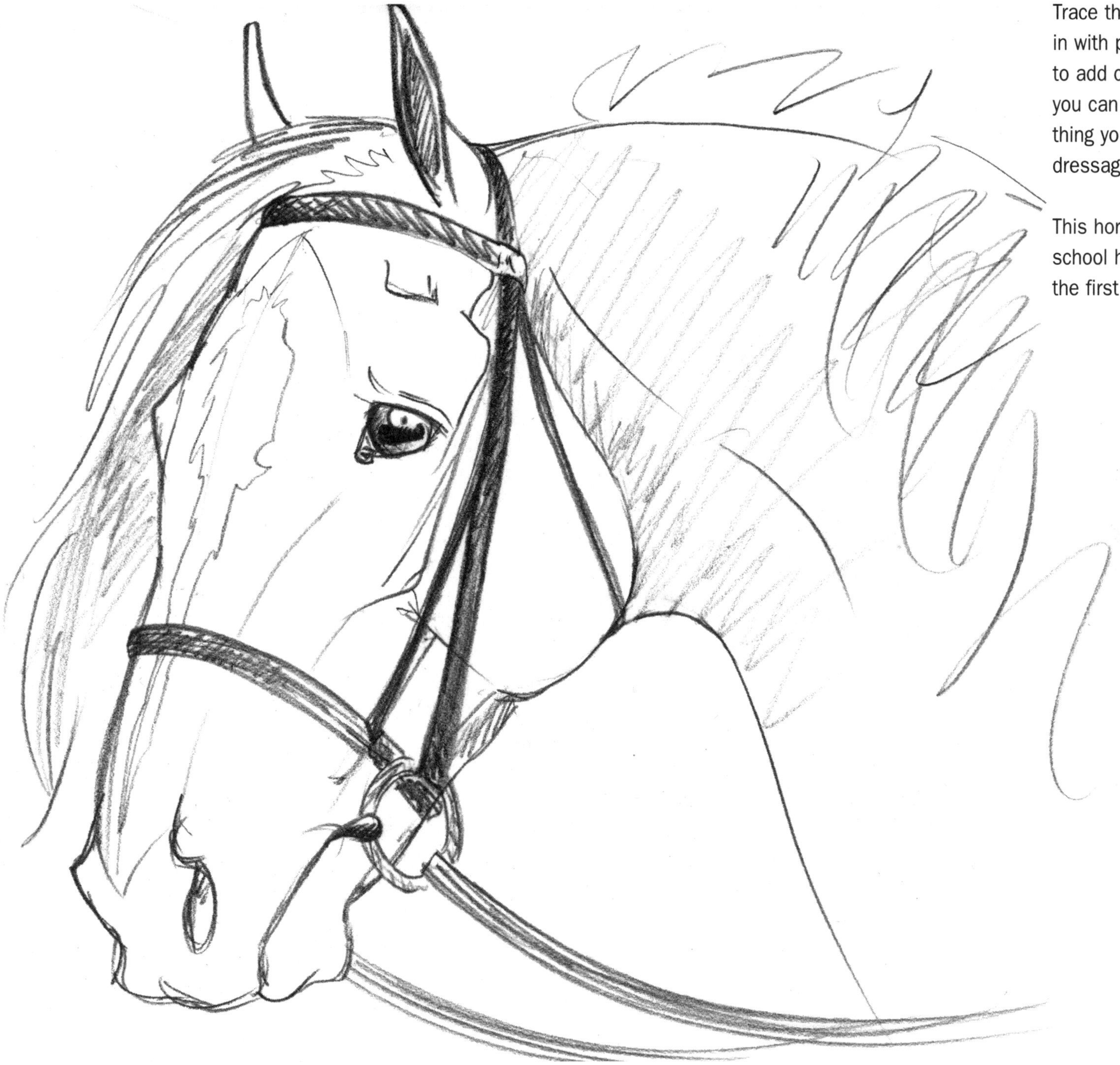

Trace this horse and shade it in with pencil, or use markers to add color. When tracing, you can change the tack to anything you want — for Western, dressage, racing or eventing.

This horse is a sweet-natured school horse waiting to give the first lesson of the day.

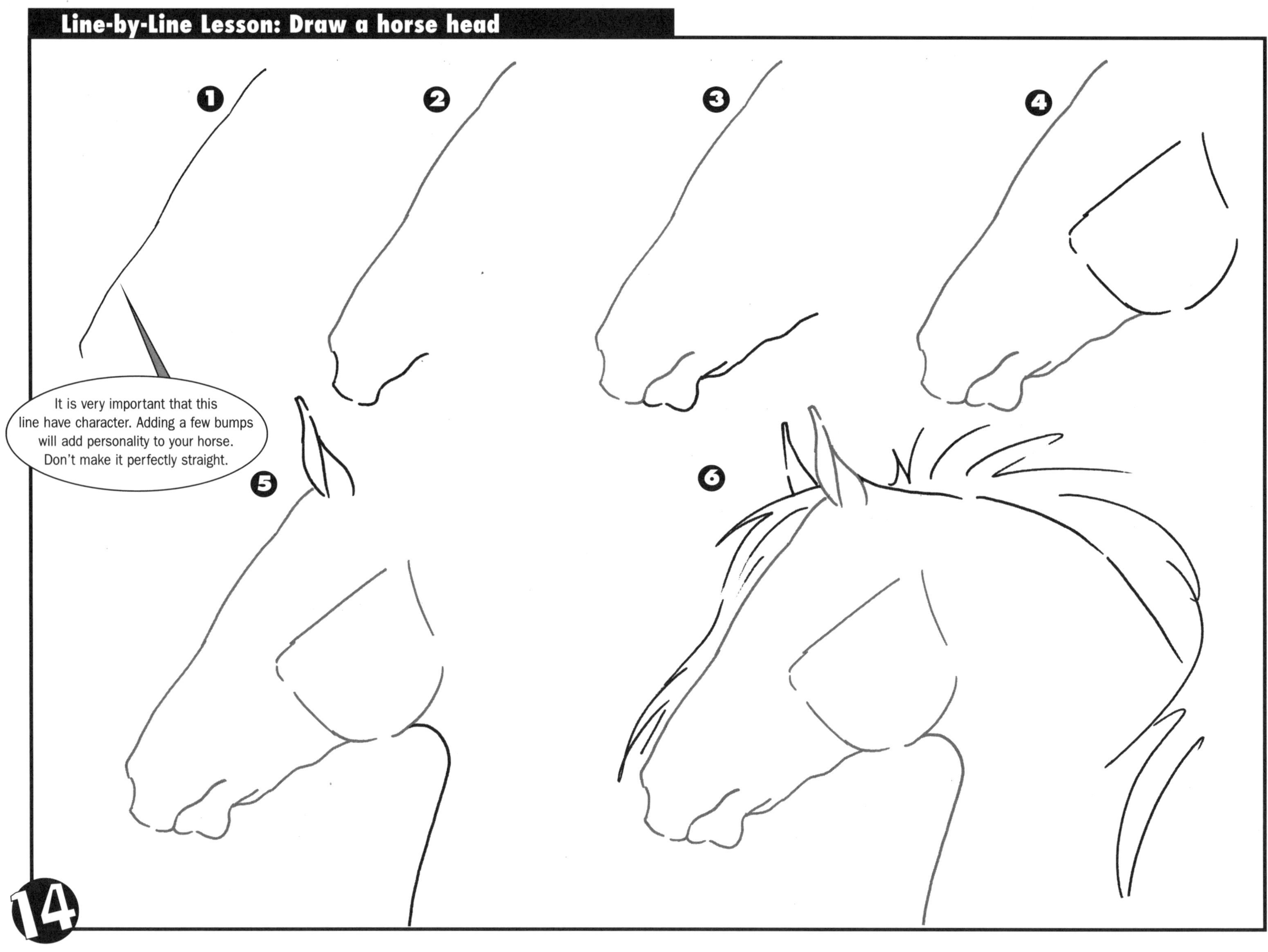
1
2
3
4
5
6
It is very important that this line have character. Adding a few bumps will add personality to your horse. Don't make it perfectly straight.

Line-by-Line Lesson: Draw a horse head

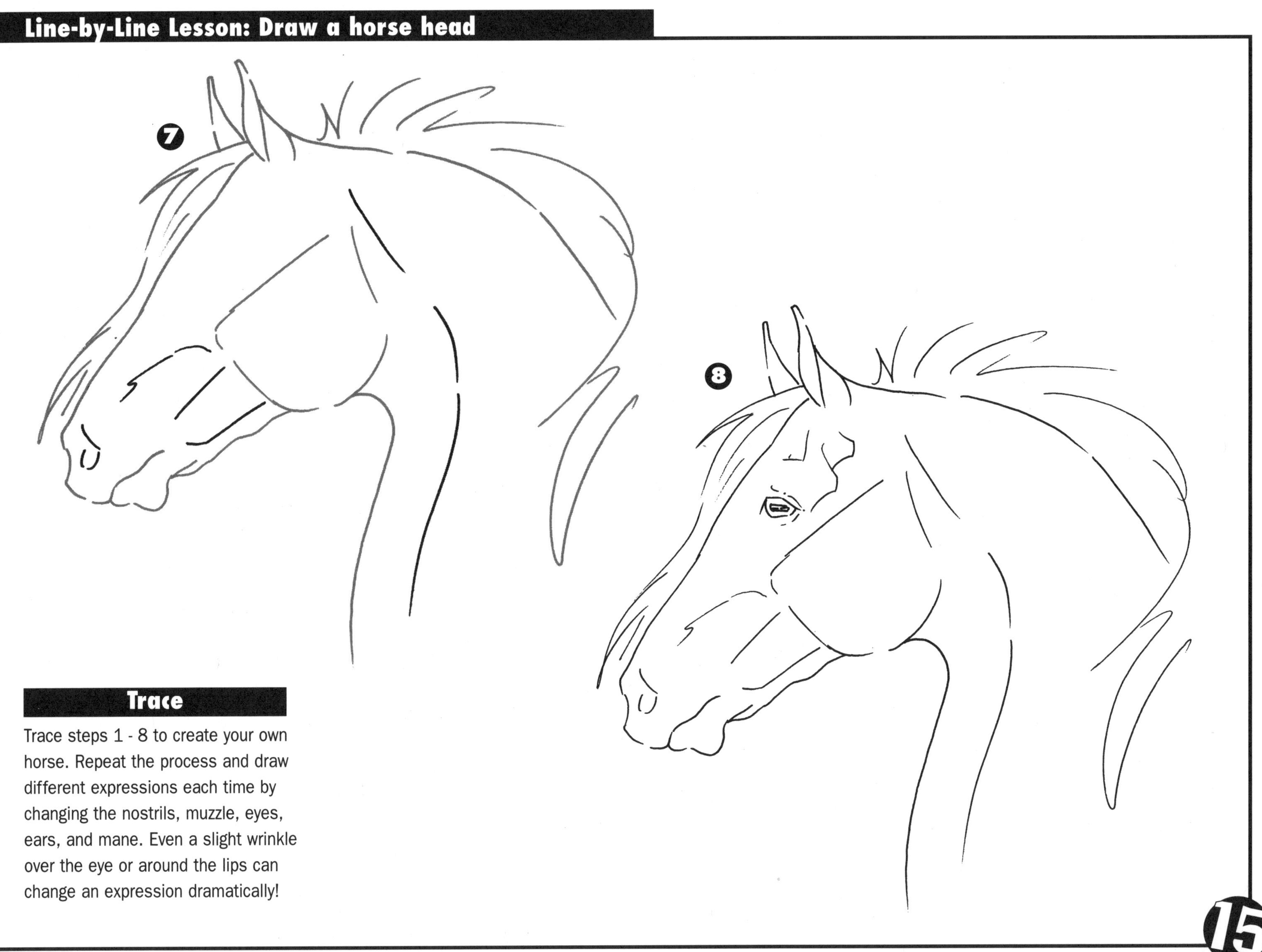

Trace

Trace steps 1 - 8 to create your own horse. Repeat the process and draw different expressions each time by changing the nostrils, muzzle, eyes, ears, and mane. Even a slight wrinkle over the eye or around the lips can change an expression dramatically!

Drawing expressions with anatomy

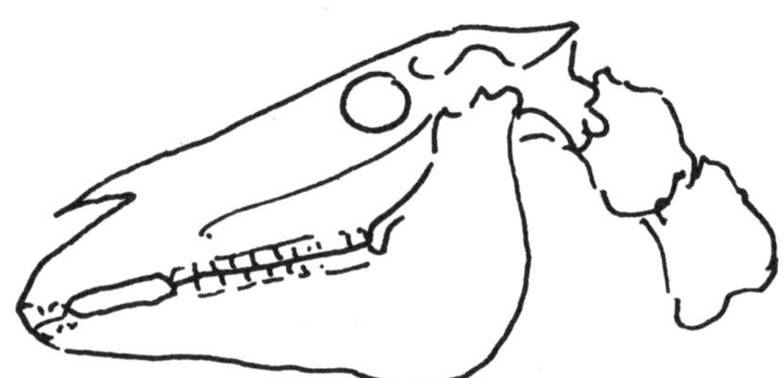

Another way to draw a horse's head is to learn the skull and form your drawing around that knowledge. This technique is the best way to draw a horse with an expression like fear and anger, where he is biting and you'll need to understand the placement of the teeth.

Above is a detailed sketch of the skull. However, when I'm drawing an angry or fearful horse, I use a very loose sketch (right) of the skull to create my head. After the skull, I sketch over a basic geometric shape to convey the horse's general shape. Then (see next page), I add the line-by-line detail of the face and the eyes and lips with the angriest expression I can conjure up.

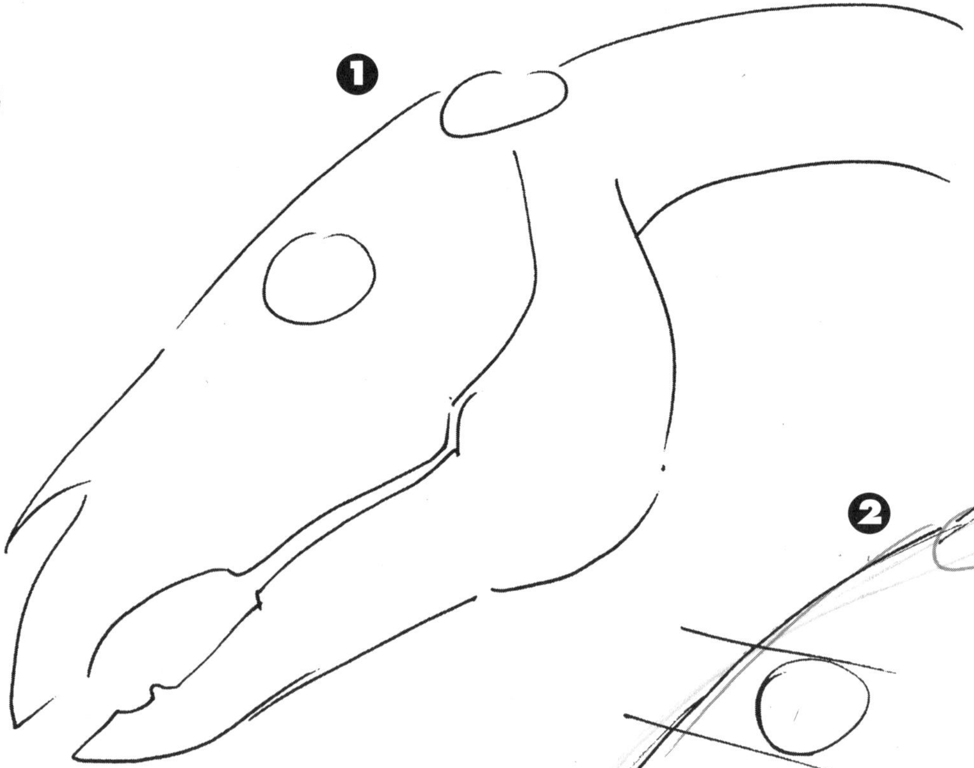

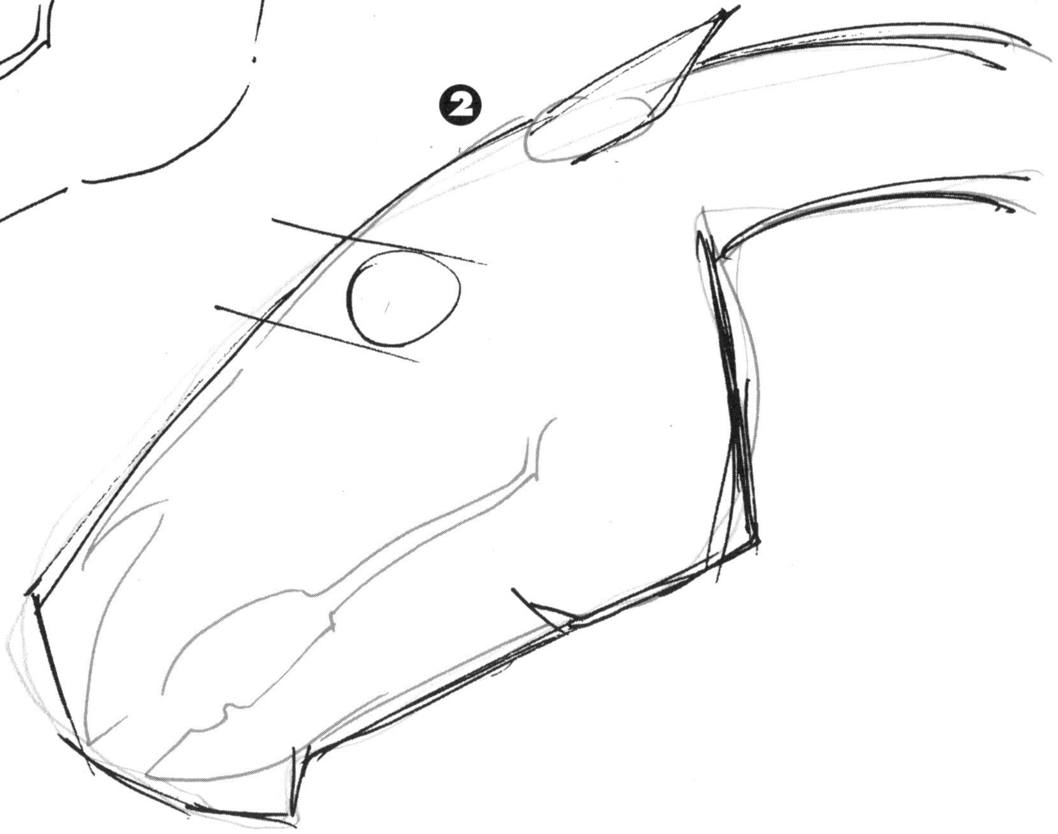

Trace

Trace heads #1 - 2 to form your horse then turn to the next page and trace #3 to finish your drawing.

...Drawing expressions

The eyes and the ears are crucial when determining the horse's expression. See pages 8 - 9 for some examples.

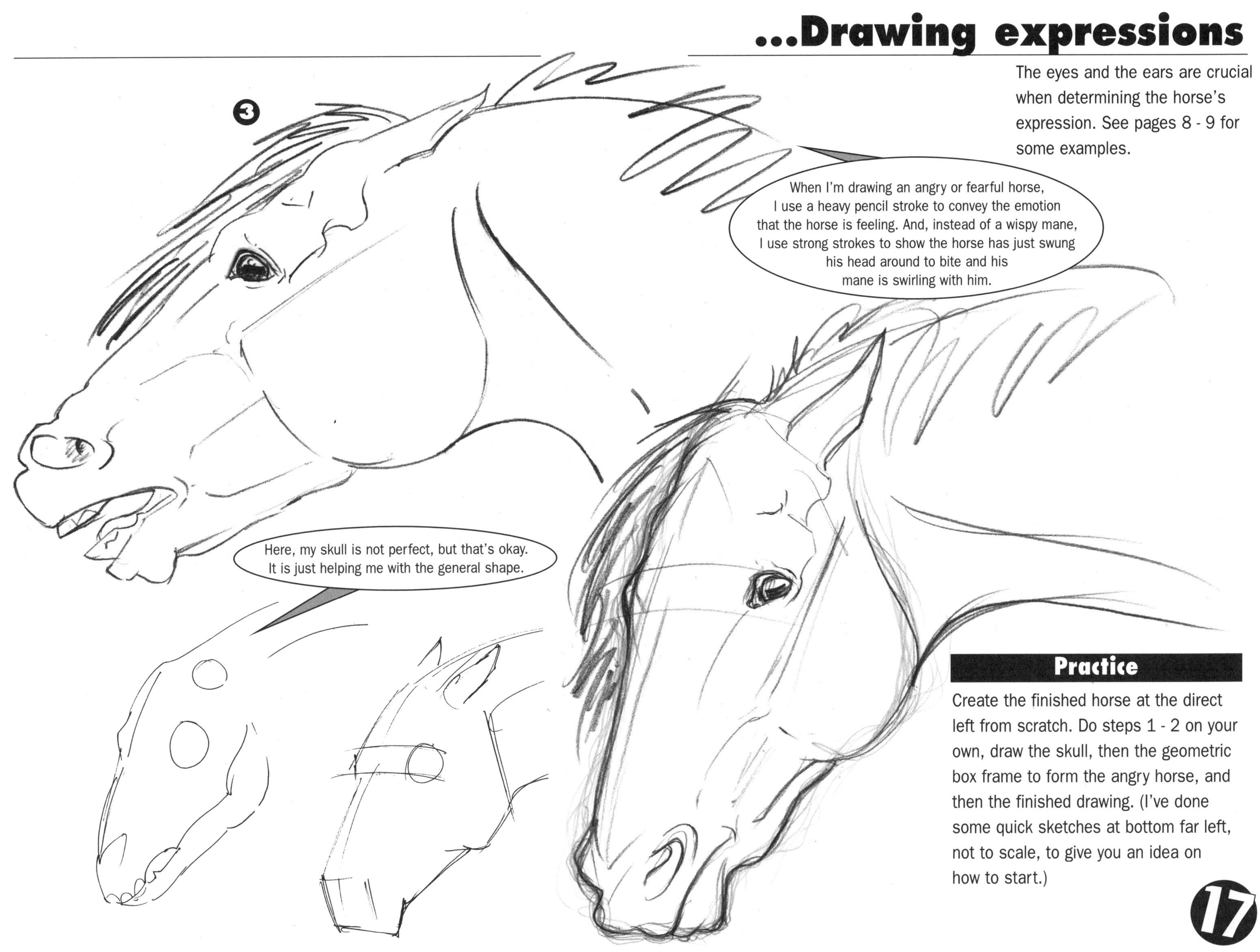

Practice

Create the finished horse at the direct left from scratch. Do steps 1 - 2 on your own, draw the skull, then the geometric box frame to form the angry horse, and then the finished drawing. (I've done some quick sketches at bottom far left, not to scale, to give you an idea on how to start.)

How to draw equipment...

Trace these heads...

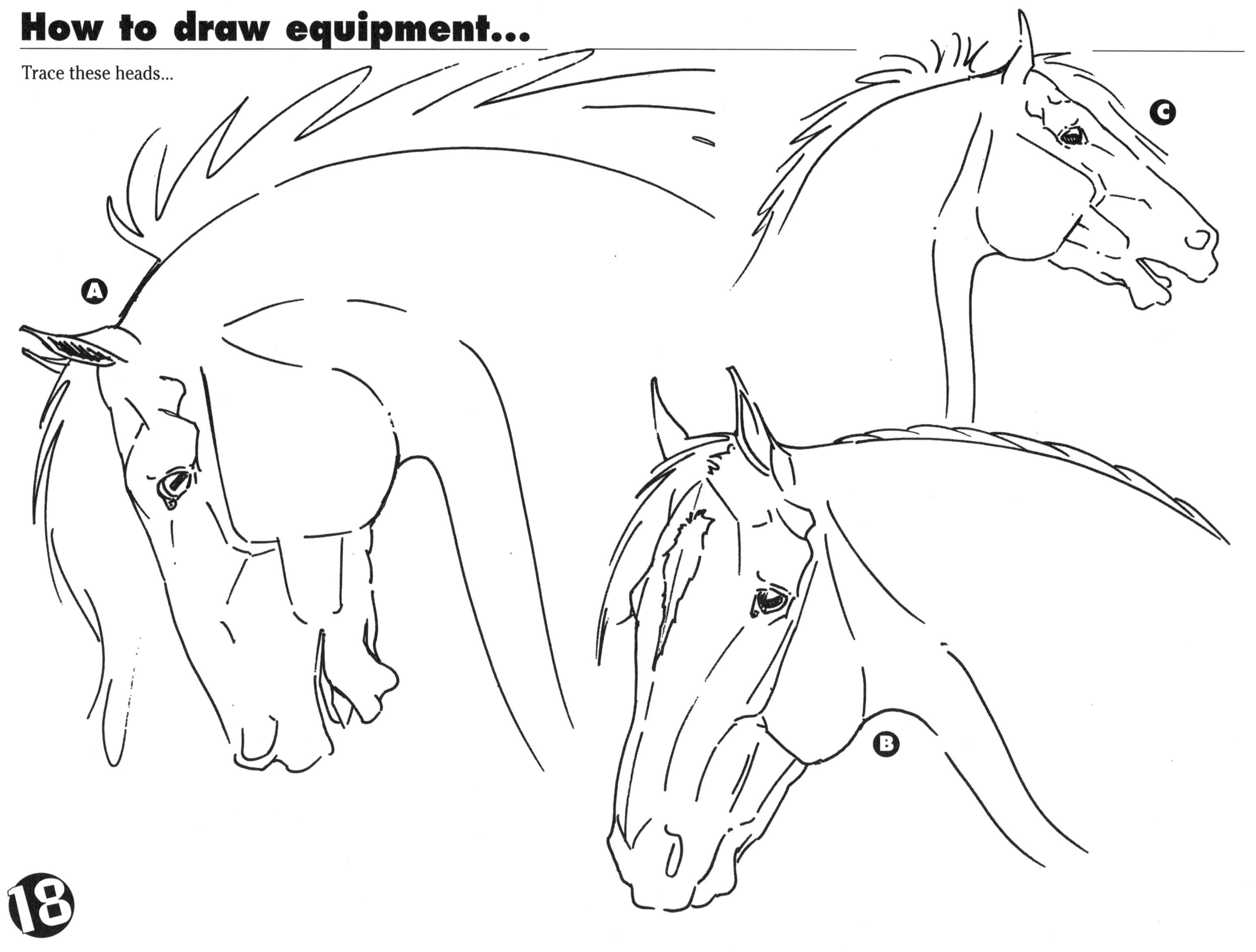

...Add a halter

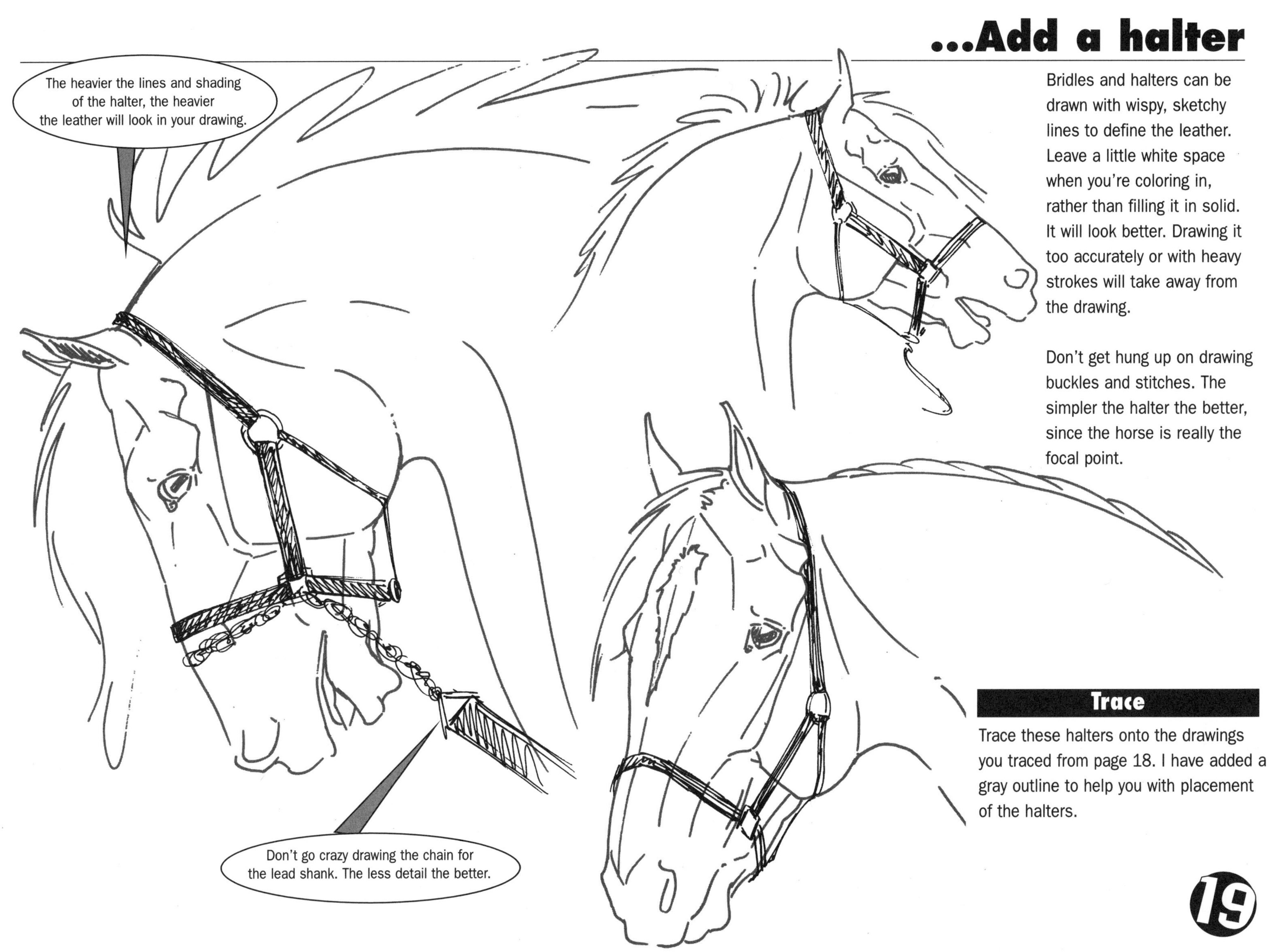

Bridles and halters can be drawn with wispy, sketchy lines to define the leather. Leave a little white space when you're coloring in, rather than filling it in solid. It will look better. Drawing it too accurately or with heavy strokes will take away from the drawing.

Don't get hung up on drawing buckles and stitches. The simpler the halter the better, since the horse is really the focal point.

Trace

Trace these halters onto the drawings you traced from page 18. I have added a gray outline to help you with placement of the halters.

...Add a bridle

It's interesting how a certain piece of tack changes the look of a horse dramatically. It's almost like the difference in a person wearing a ball gown and a t-shirt and jeans. Try the different bridles at right and below on the horses you've drawn, or create your own. Save equine supply catalogs or stop by your local tack store to research the various bridles and bits.

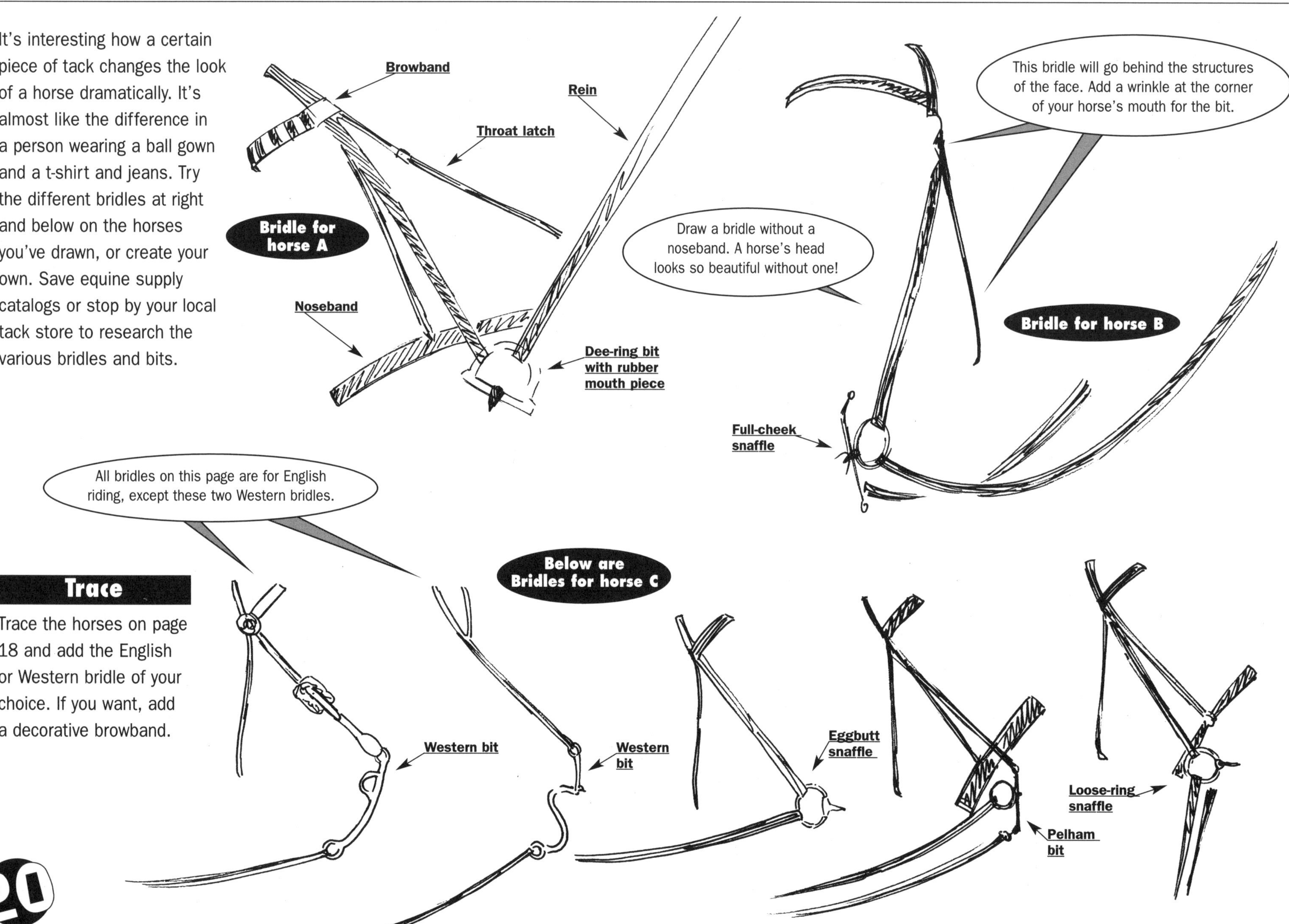

Trace

Trace the horses on page 18 and add the English or Western bridle of your choice. If you want, add a decorative browband.

DRAWING THE

Horse's Body

in 4 easy steps!

Gestures:

When I draw the body of a horse, I start with a loose gesture. Scribble the energy that you feel is in the horse you're about to draw. Even this standing horse has movement. The movement here is in which leg is bearing more weight.

Practice and practice on gestures. It will make your drawings better and better.

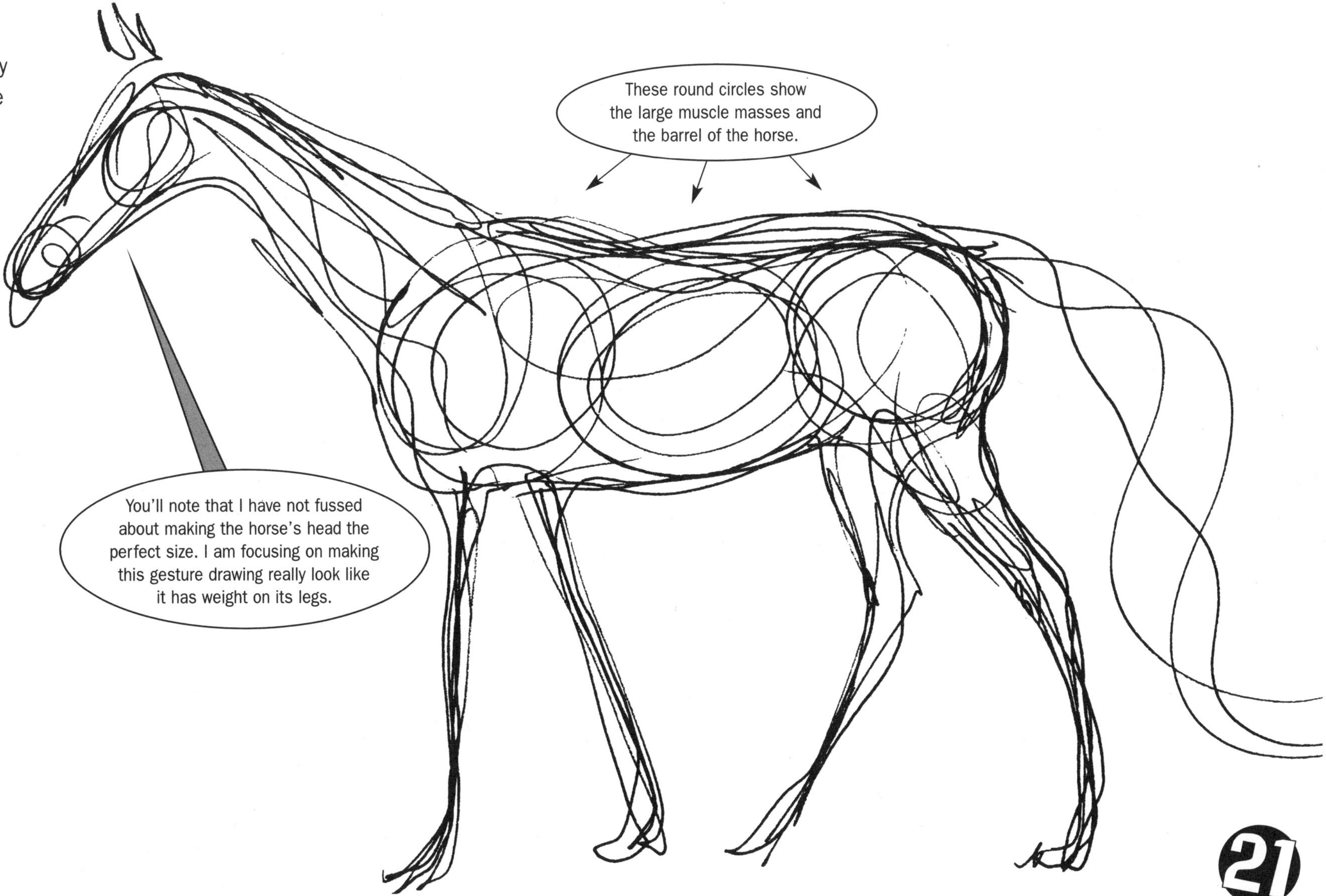

Trace

Trace the gesture stages on pages 21 - 23.

The horse's body...

Don't worry about making mistakes at this stage. Use your eye to get the length of the legs, body, and head. You will be correcting and adjusting as you progress through your drawing. Right now, you want your horse to appear to be really standing with weight on his legs. Make your lines heavier if they are "supporting" the horse's weight. Practice your gesture until you feel you have the motion down pat. Then proceed to page 23.

Experiment

When I'm drawing a horse's head, I prefer to use the geometrical approach. However, try drawing your own horse head by starting with a gesture. This may work better for you.

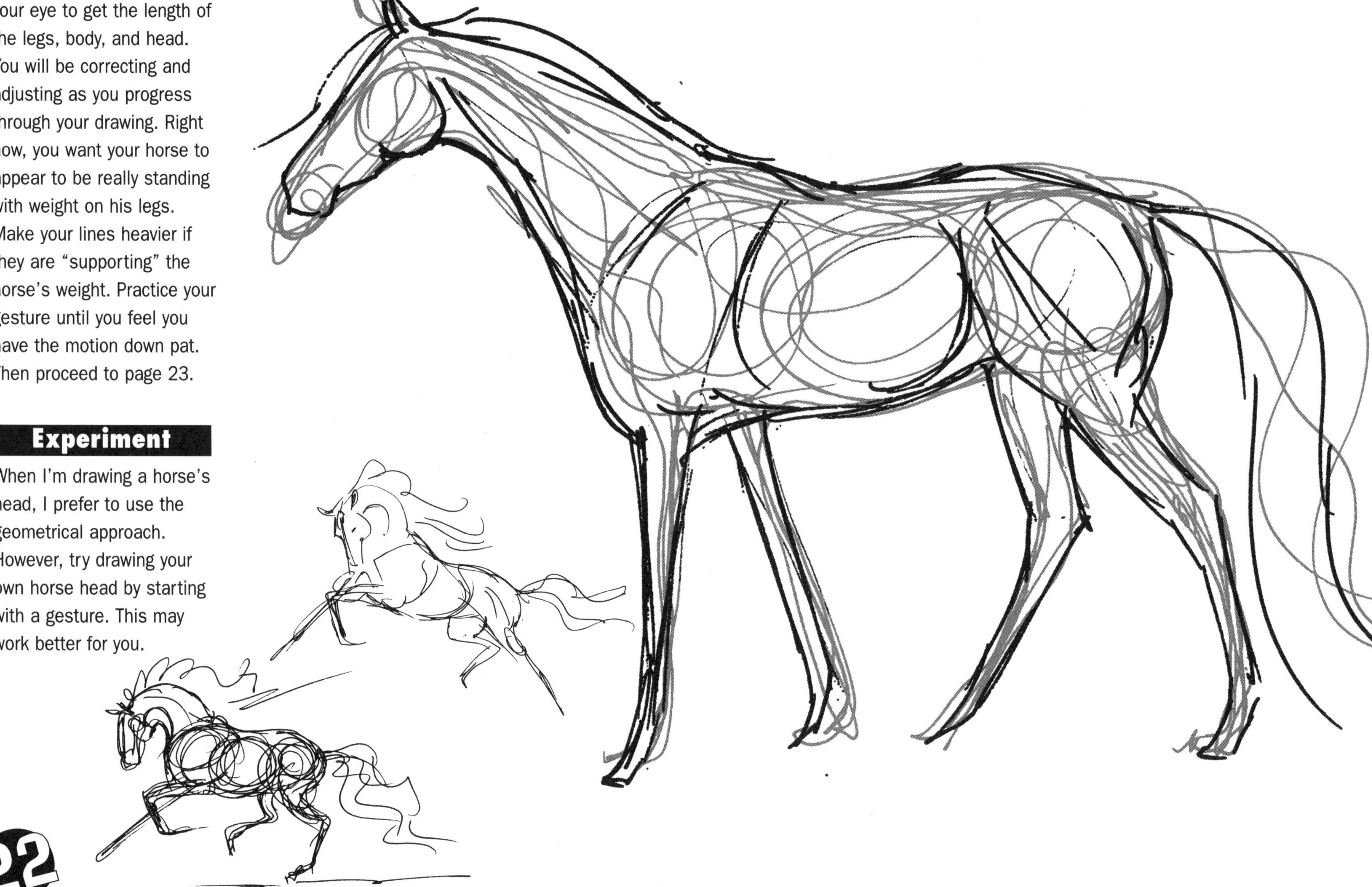

...Add the details

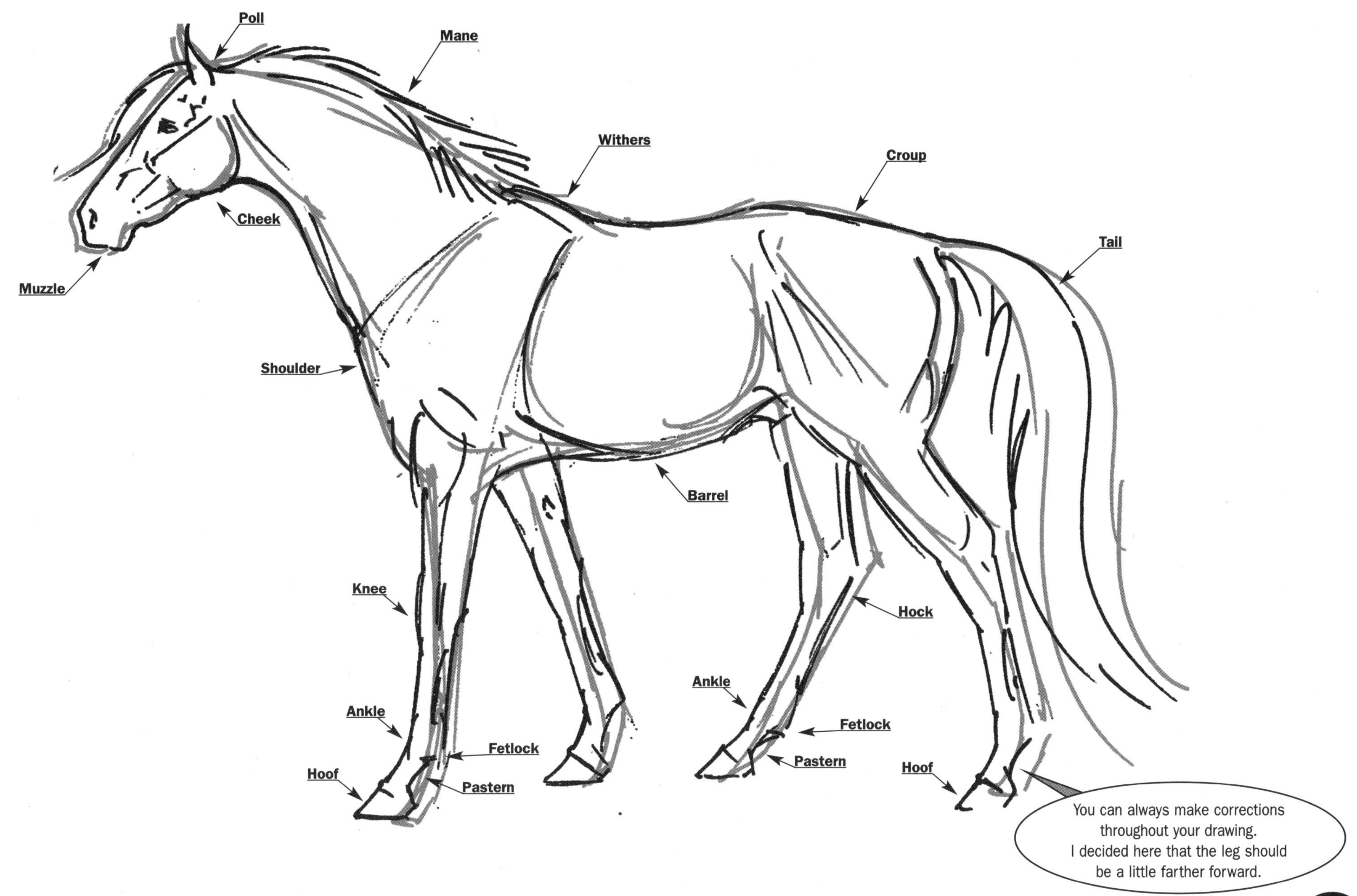

...Add shading

Practice with different mediums (pencils, pens, inks, etc.) to shade in. Use this horse and its shading as a guide to create your own masterpiece.

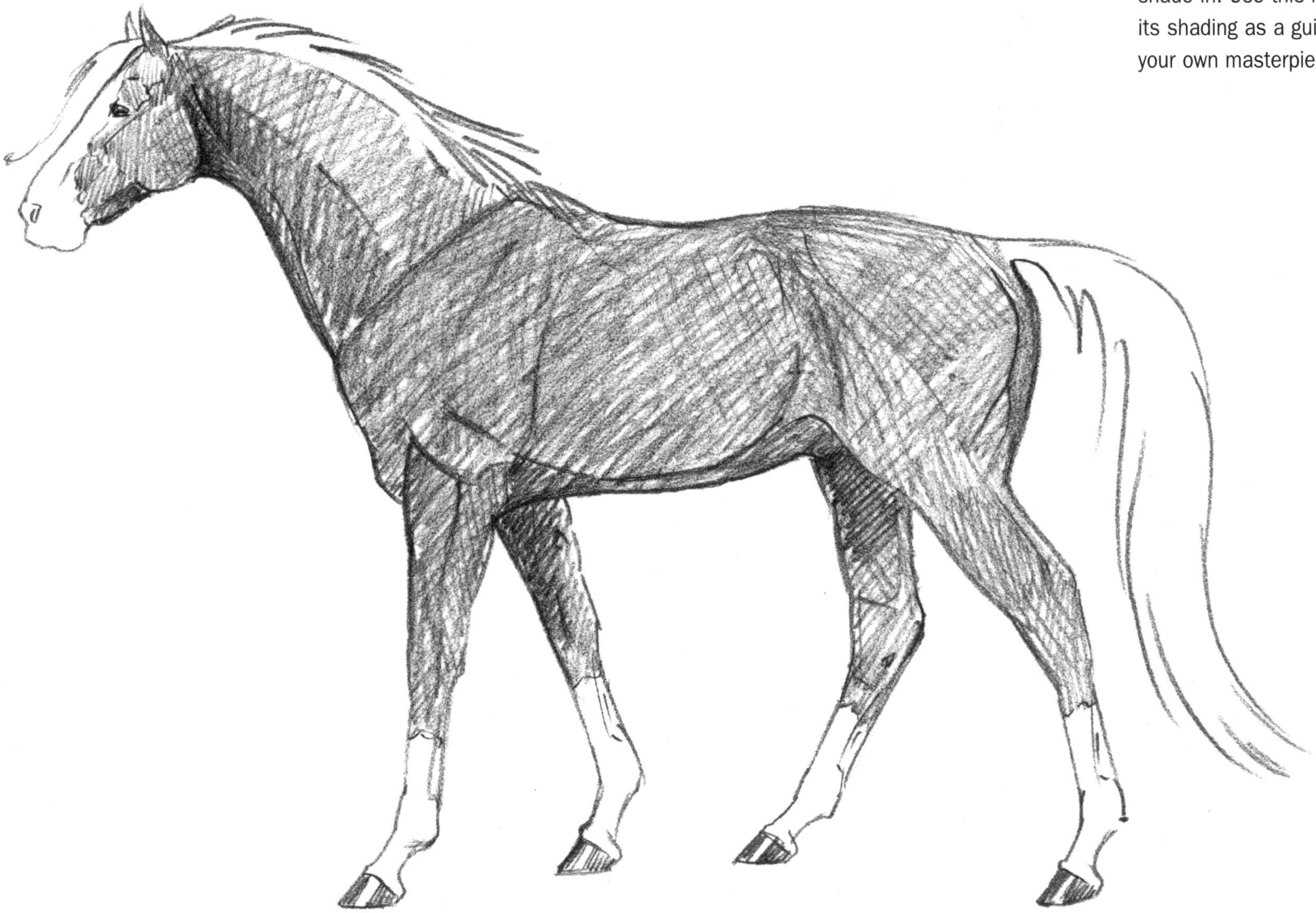

Trace

It's fun to draw different equipment on your horse. Use the horse from the previous page to "saddle up" with these traceable models.

Remember, for best results use sketchy lines for reins, leathers, and girths. Drawing them too accurately will take away from the actual drawing of the horse.

Is your horse going cross country or trail riding? Add leg wraps or boots from page 38 to complete your picture. Refer to equine catalogs to get even more equipment ideas.

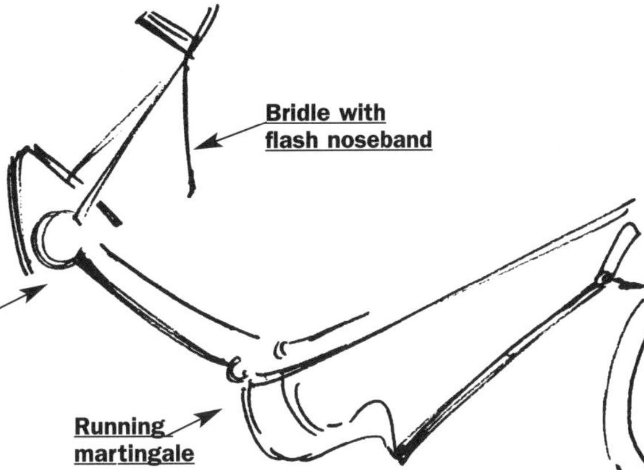

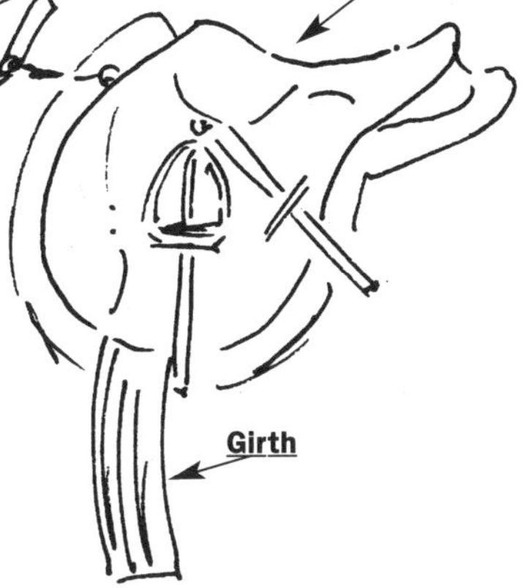

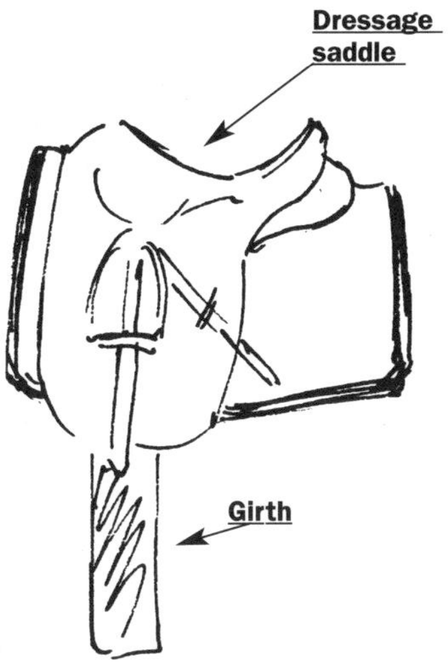

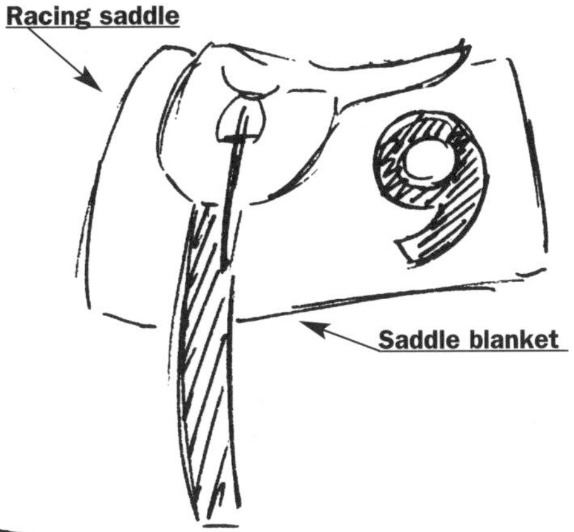

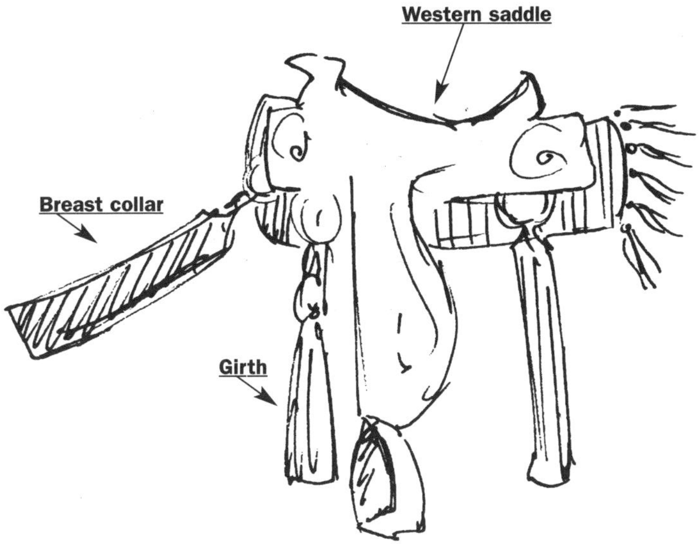

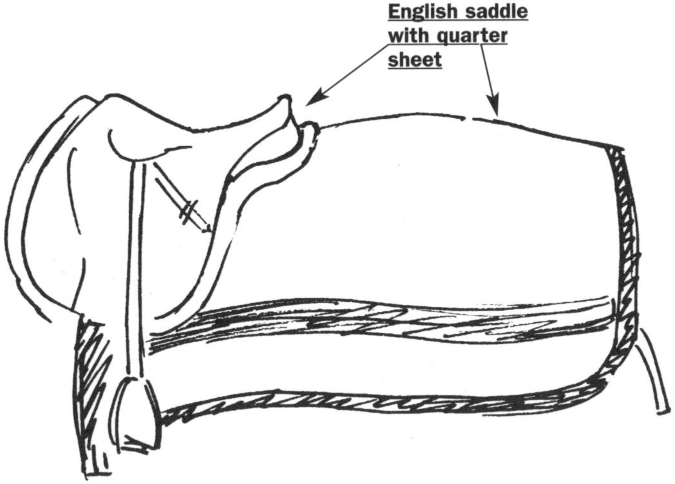

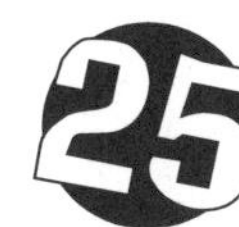

...Add a little movement and trot him out!

Trace

You can trace the saddles from the previous page onto this horse and the horses on the next few pages.

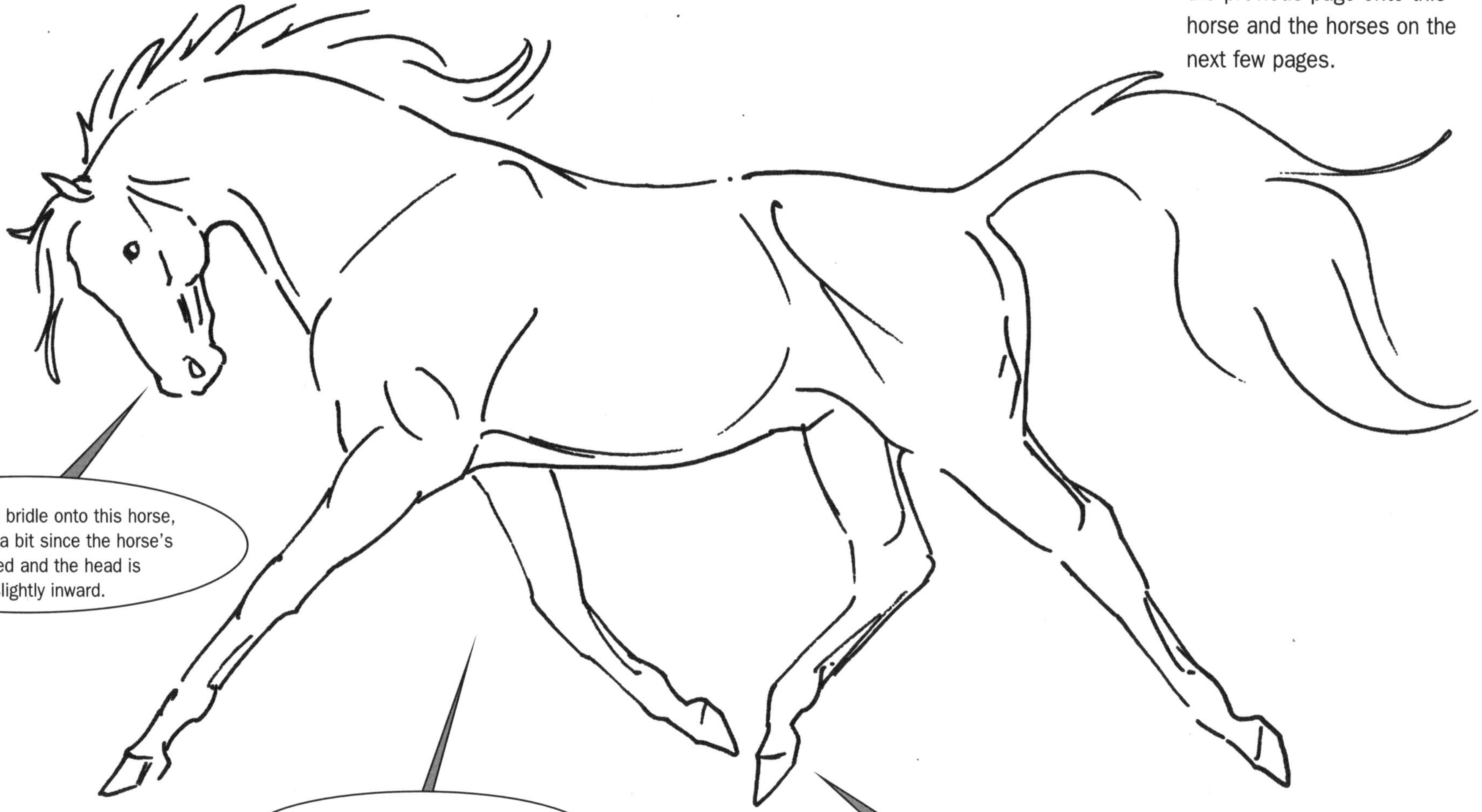

When you trace a bridle onto this horse, adjust the bridle a bit since the horse's neck is arched and the head is turned slightly inward.

Draw a Baker™ blanket on this horse with the models on pages 31 - 32.

Notice these simplified hooves.
Don't get too intricate in drawing them, especially when the focal point of this drawing is the expression of a happy horse trotting off.

Practice

Trace these horses and practice shading. Try different techniques: cross-hatching, using your finger to smudge the pencil, or painting.

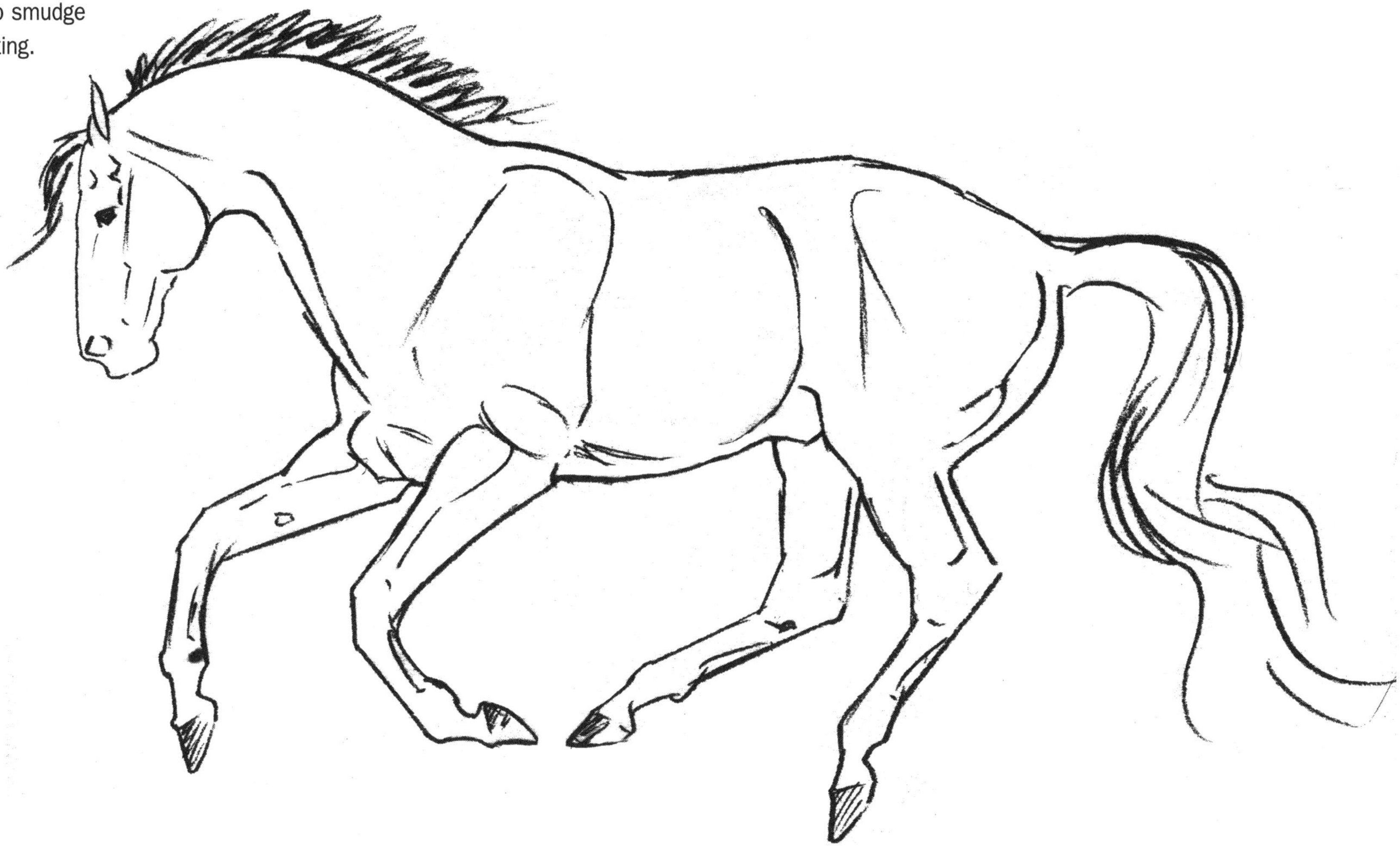

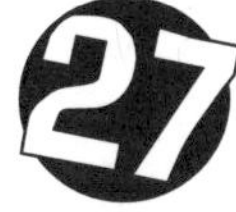

...Try a jumping scene

For this kind of action shot and the bucking horse on page 34, practice your gesture drawing first so you can give the horse the swoop of energy going over the fence, or plant the "weight" of the horse in his buck to the ground.

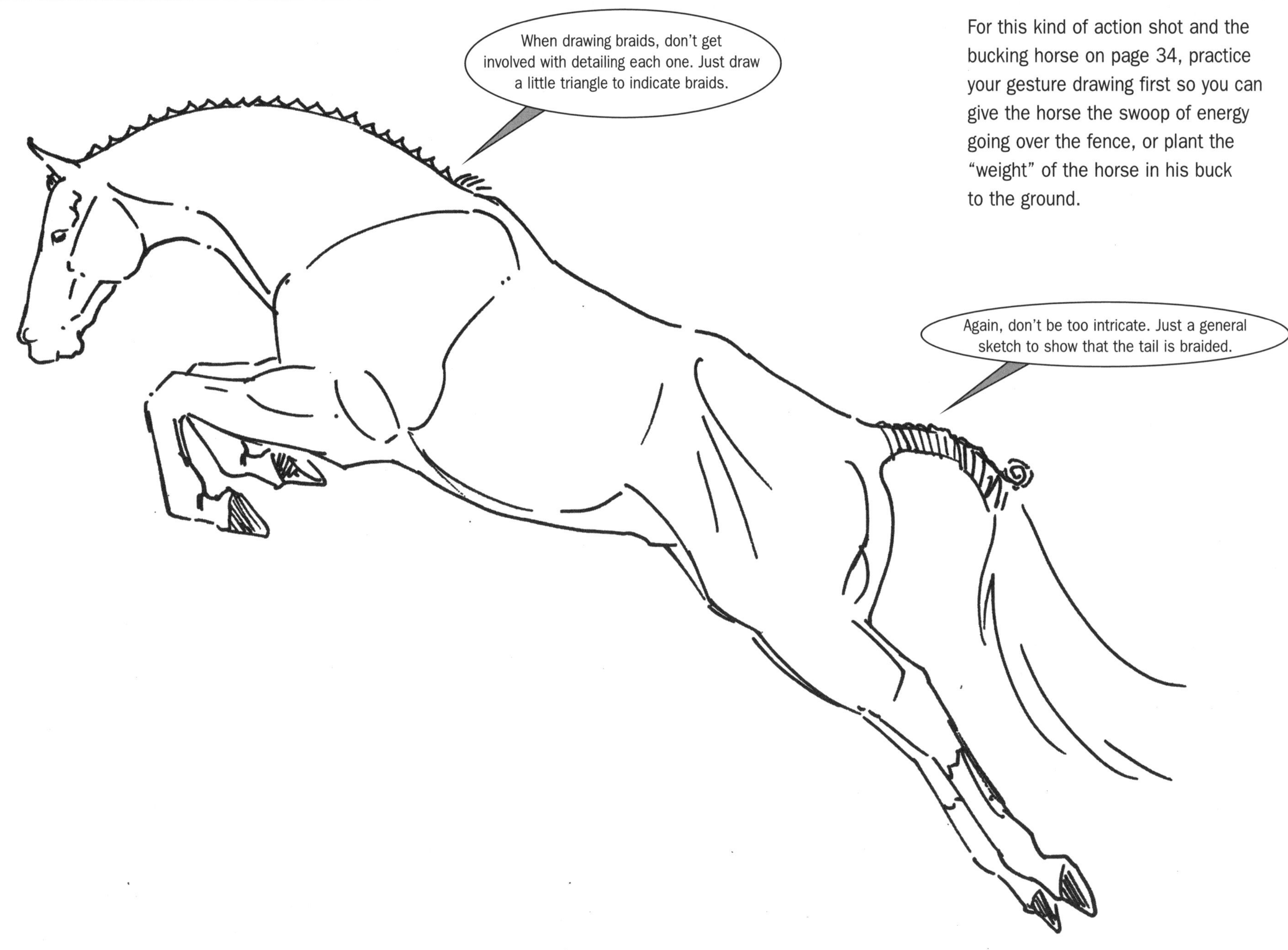

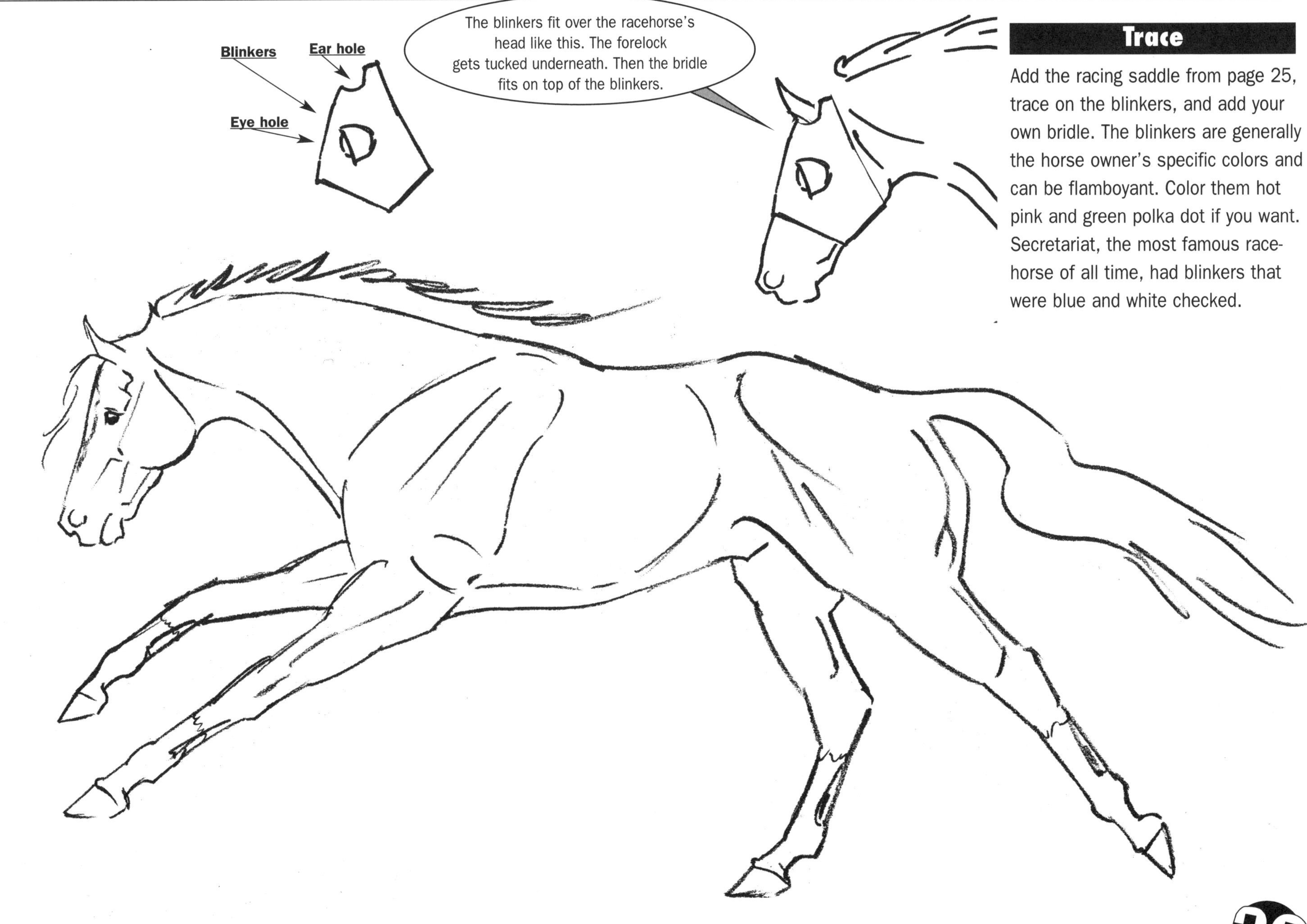

Trace

Add the racing saddle from page 25, trace on the blinkers, and add your own bridle. The blinkers are generally the horse owner's specific colors and can be flamboyant. Color them hot pink and green polka dot if you want. Secretariat, the most famous racehorse of all time, had blinkers that were blue and white checked.

Put a little perspective on things...

When you are drawing a horse in perspective (where you want his hind legs to look farther back than his front legs), draw two lines to a point on a horizon line and attach the horse's hooves to these lines. This will make your horse look like he is really planted on the ground. It gives your drawing more credibility.

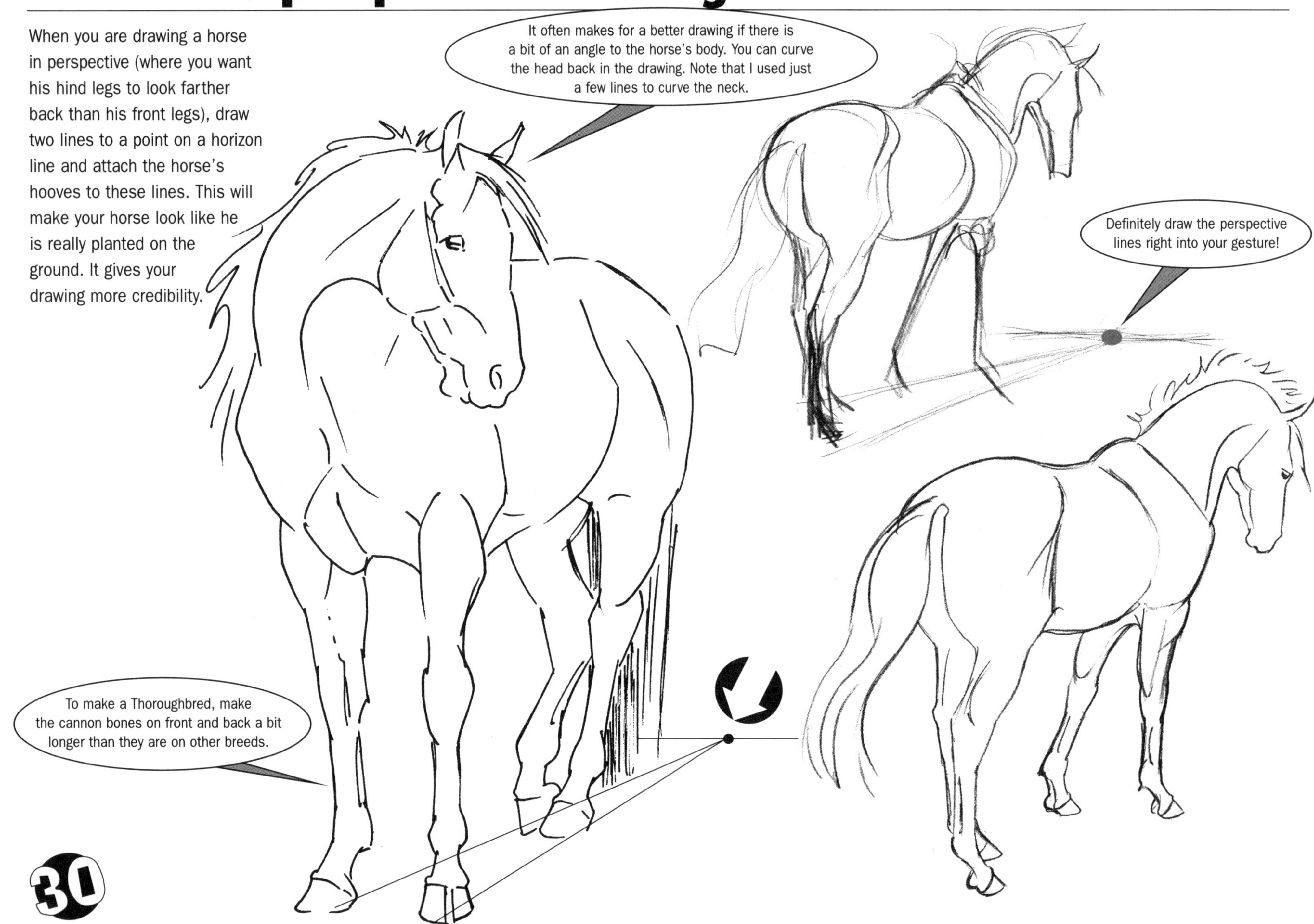

...Add a Baker™ blanket

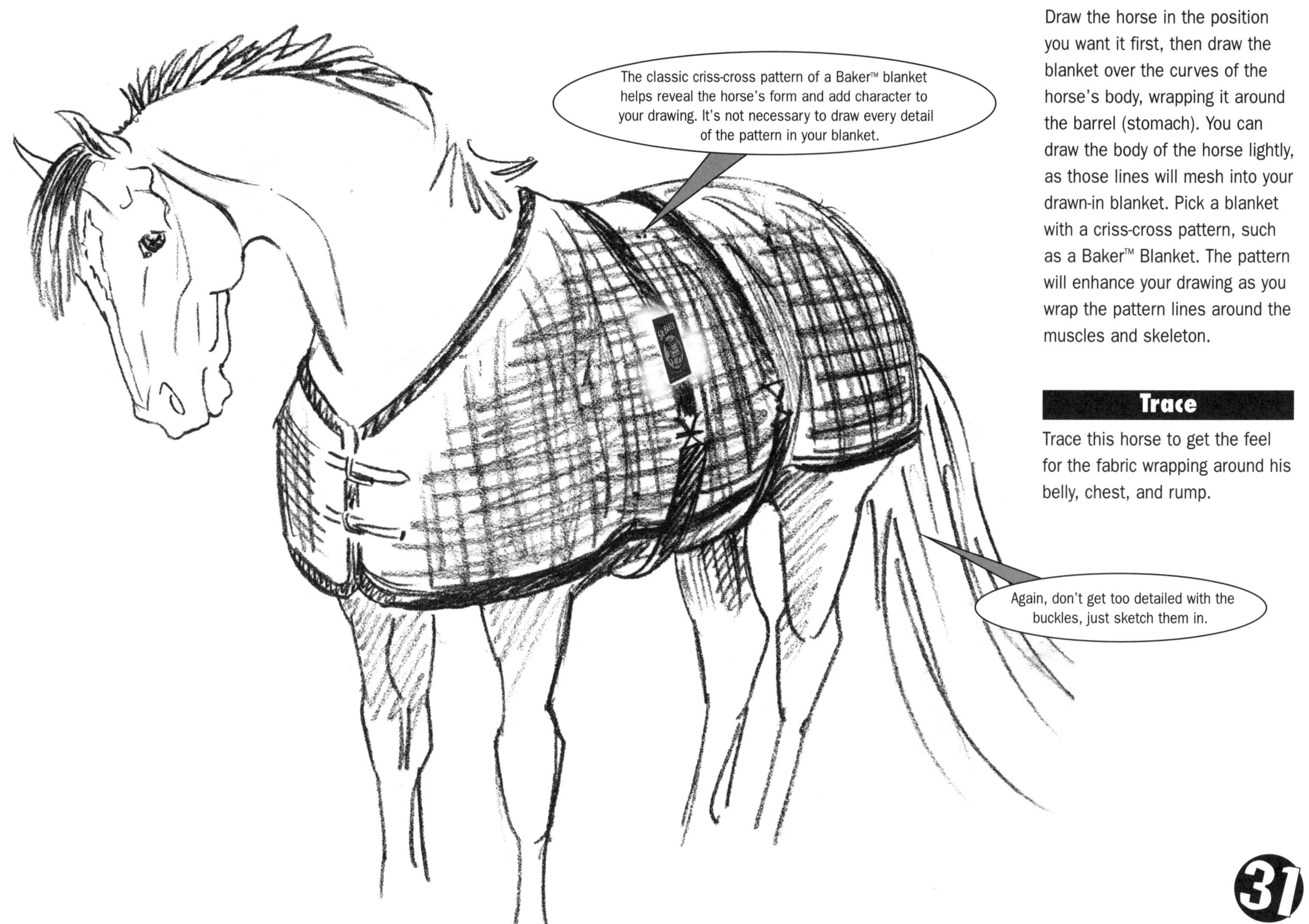

Draw the horse in the position you want it first, then draw the blanket over the curves of the horse's body, wrapping it around the barrel (stomach). You can draw the body of the horse lightly, as those lines will mesh into your drawn-in blanket. Pick a blanket with a criss-cross pattern, such as a Baker™ Blanket. The pattern will enhance your drawing as you wrap the pattern lines around the muscles and skeleton.

Trace

Trace this horse to get the feel for the fabric wrapping around his belly, chest, and rump.

...Add a Baker™ blanket

Follow the dotted line to create the blanket on this horse, and change it into different blankets by using texture. Try drawing a polar fleece cooler, fly sheet, heavy winter blanket, etc. Again, stop by your local tack store or pick up an equine catalog or go to www.bakerblankets.com.

The horse at right is excited about being turned out. Whoa, boy! Add a halter and lead to slow him down.

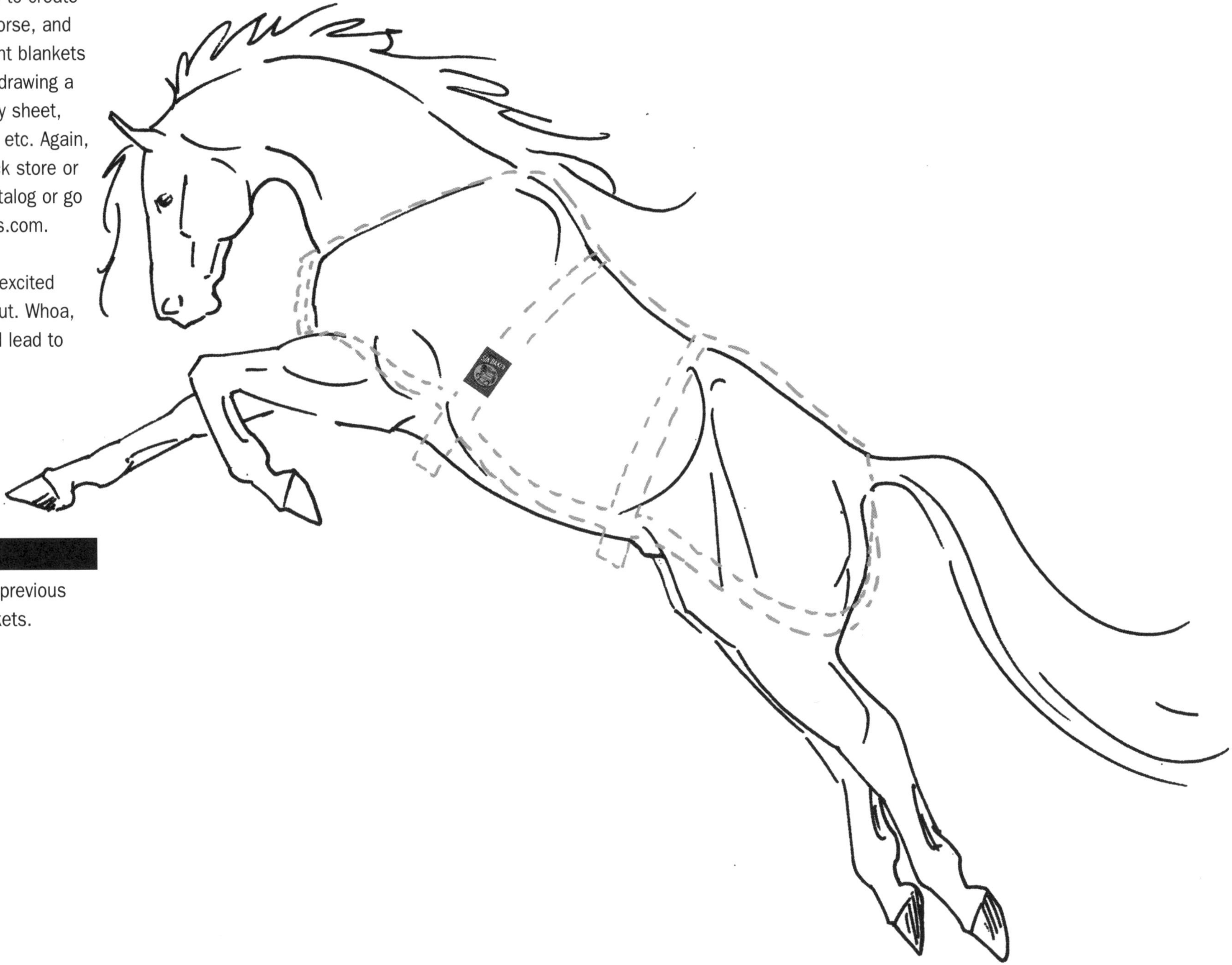

Trace

Trace the horses on previous pages and add blankets.

...Then turn him out!

When a horse is grazing, it becomes apparent how really big his head is. The head will usually measure from the ground to his knees. I'll rough out a gesture to get the proportions correct.

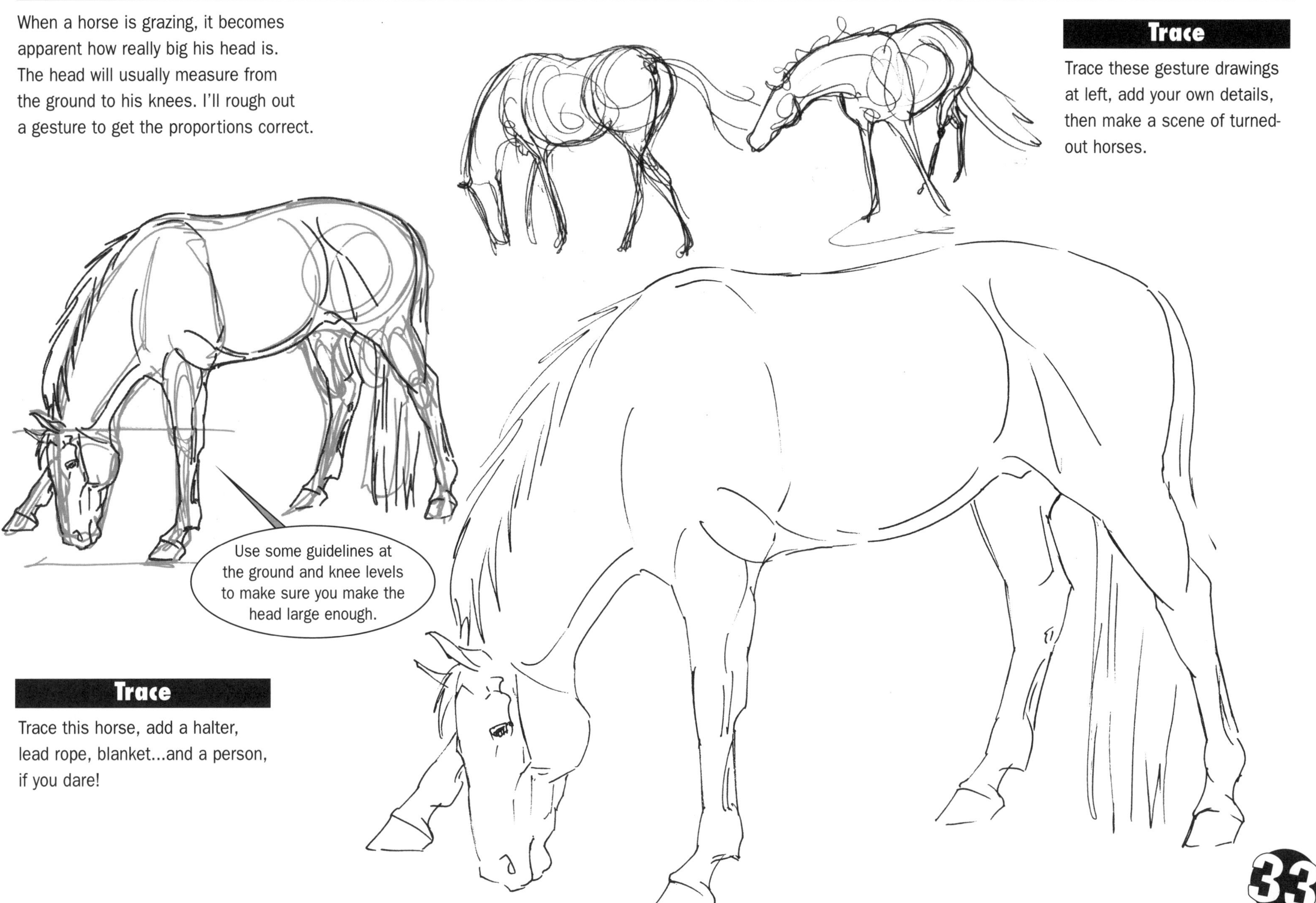

Trace

Trace these gesture drawings at left, add your own details, then make a scene of turned-out horses.

Trace

Trace this horse, add a halter, lead rope, blanket...and a person, if you dare!

...And watch him buck!

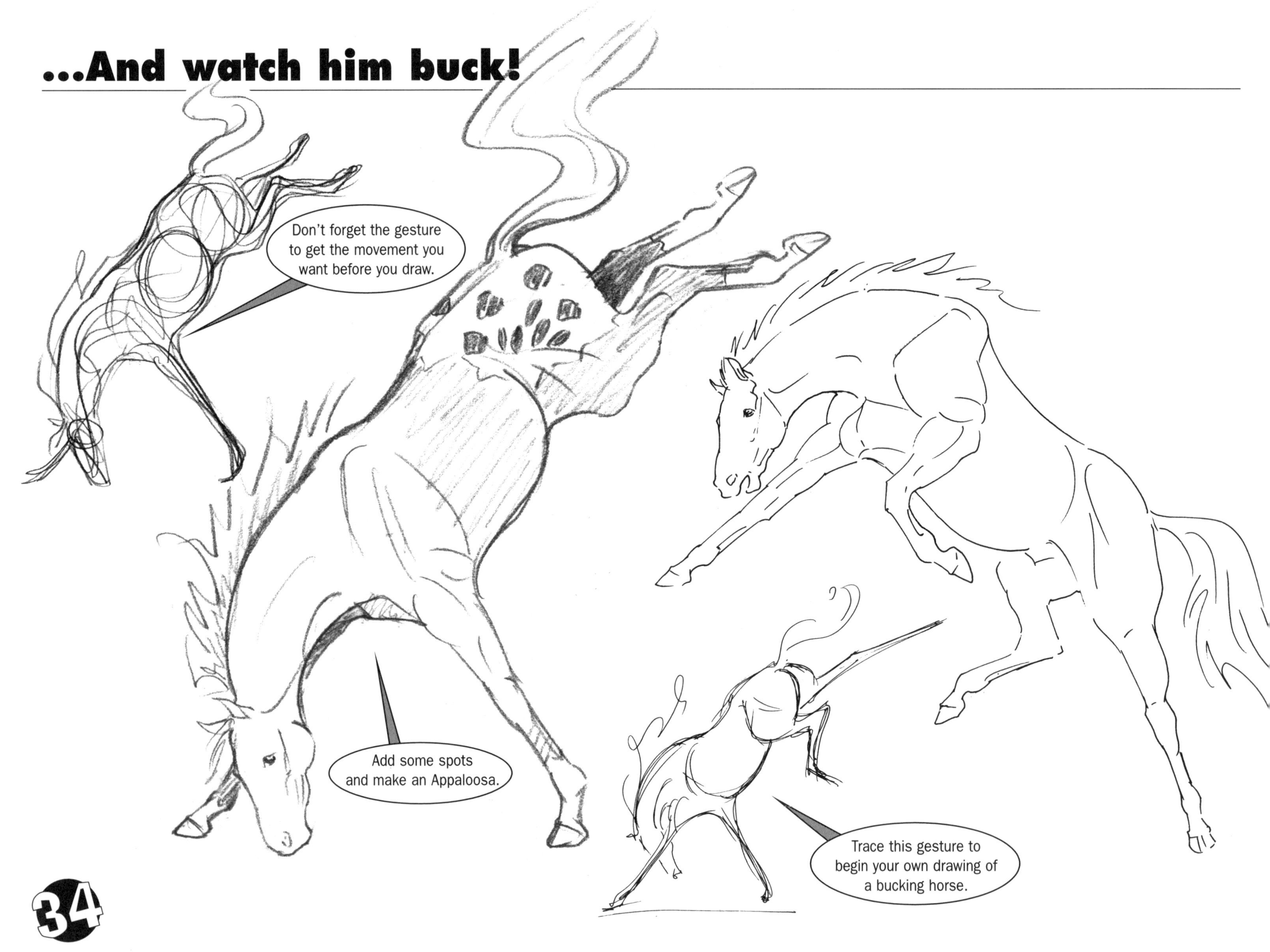

Legs & Hooves just right!

One way to draw legs is to use a very simple version of the gesture to sketch in the movement, then sketch geometric shapes to represent the knee, forearm, ankle and hoof. Then streamline your geometric shapes to create the muscles and skin over the legs and belly.

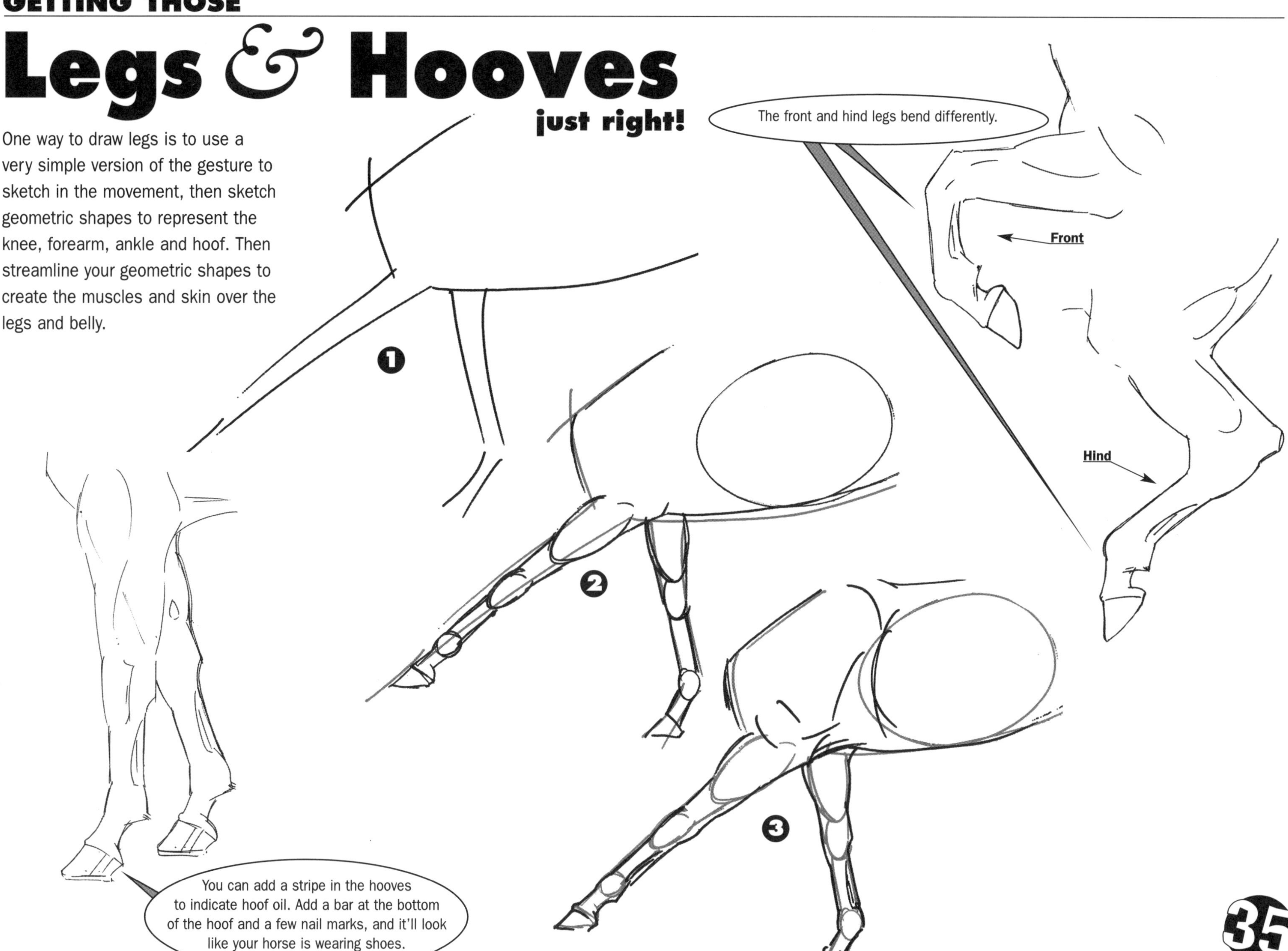

...Legs, legs & more legs

Trace

Trace sketch #3 from page 35 and connect it with #3 from this page to create a running horse. Use what you have learned to draw the horse's head on your own.

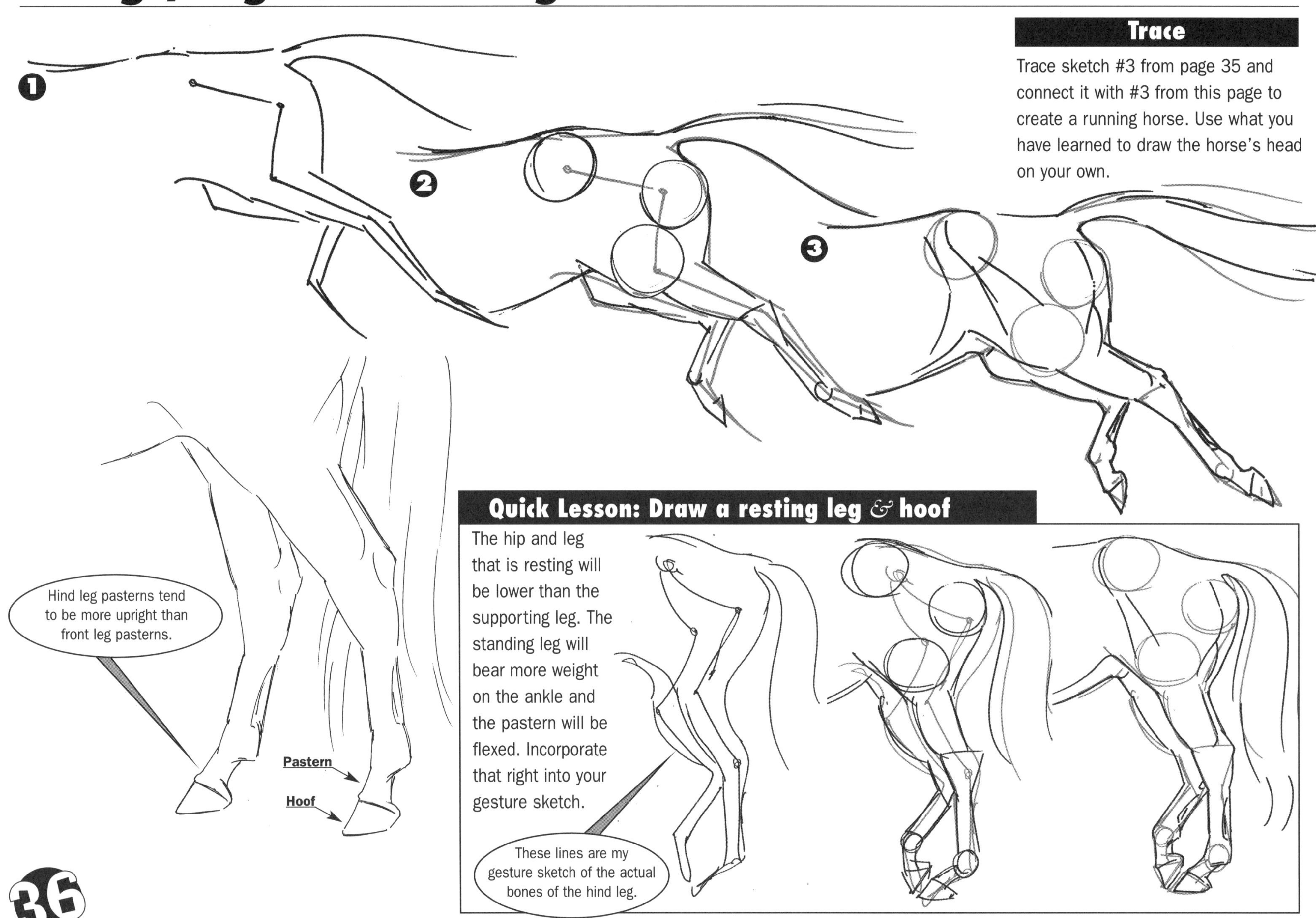

Quick Lesson: Draw a resting leg & hoof

The hip and leg that is resting will be lower than the supporting leg. The standing leg will bear more weight on the ankle and the pastern will be flexed. Incorporate that right into your gesture sketch.

The hardest thing to draw is the hoof. It helps if you break it down to a few simple lines and geometric shapes. Use less detail and your drawing will be more believable.

Trace

Trace these shapes and draw your own hoof as I have done.

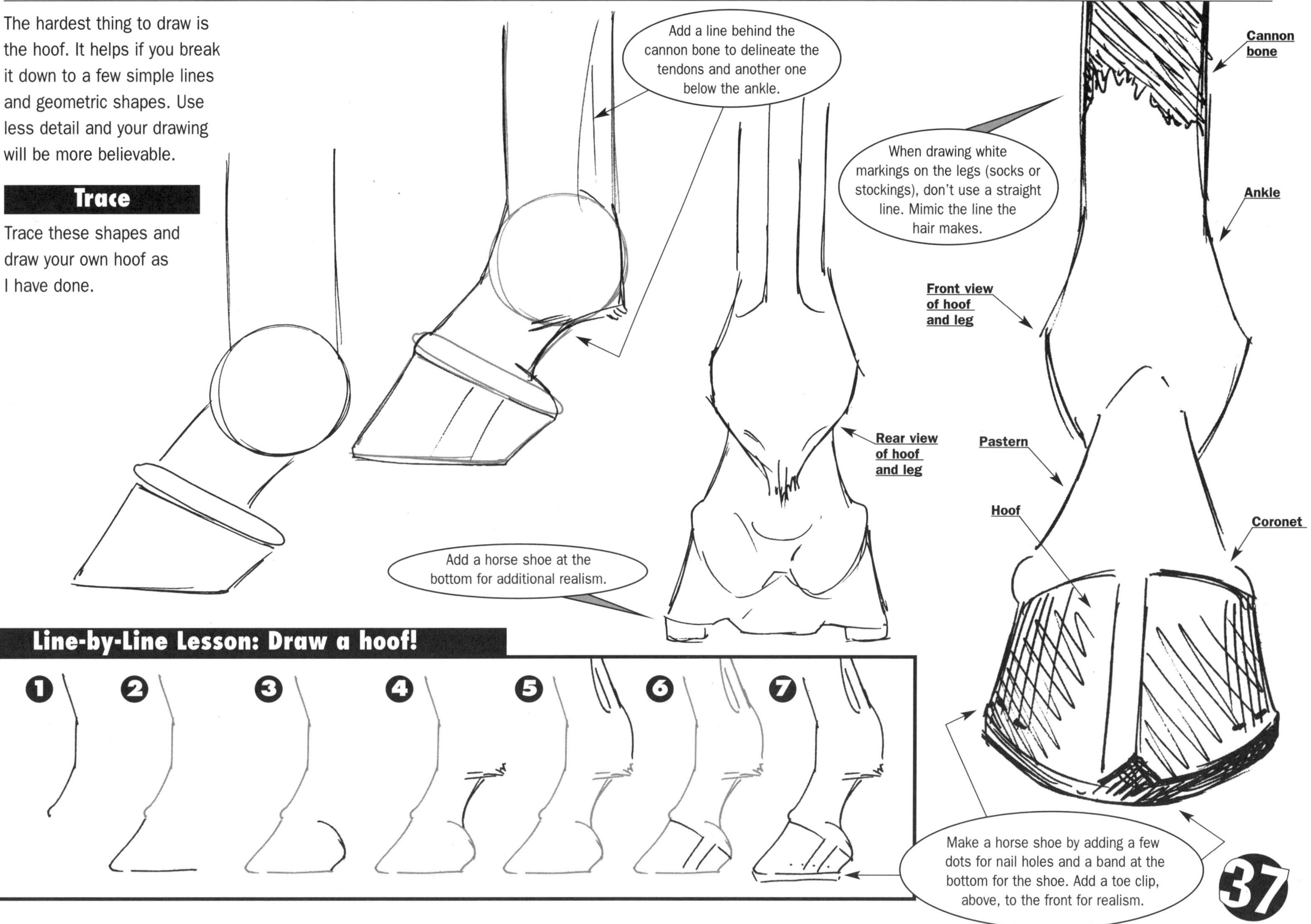

...Add equipment

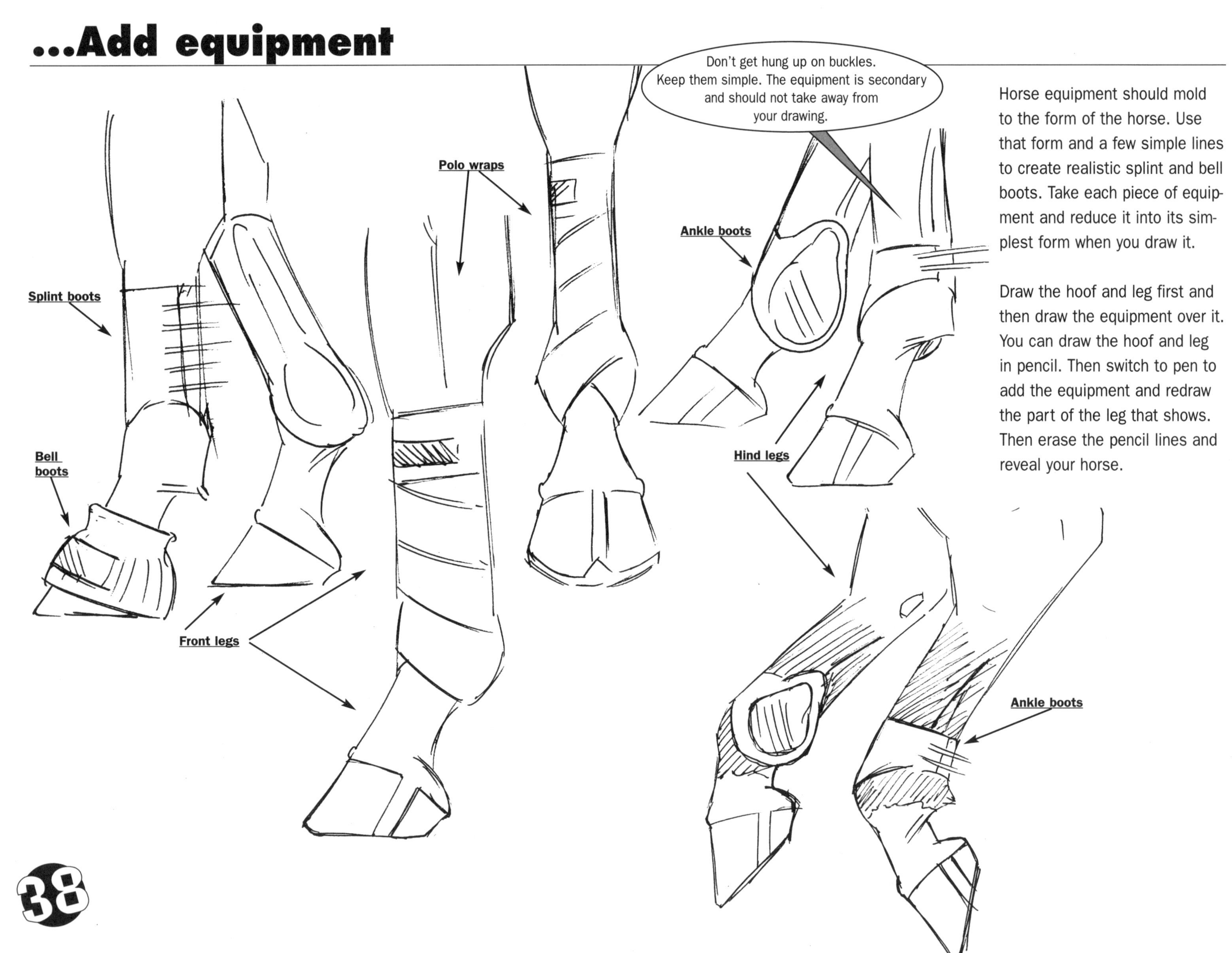

Horse equipment should mold to the form of the horse. Use that form and a few simple lines to create realistic splint and bell boots. Take each piece of equipment and reduce it into its simplest form when you draw it.

Draw the hoof and leg first and then draw the equipment over it. You can draw the hoof and leg in pencil. Then switch to pen to add the equipment and redraw the part of the leg that shows. Then erase the pencil lines and reveal your horse.

Finale

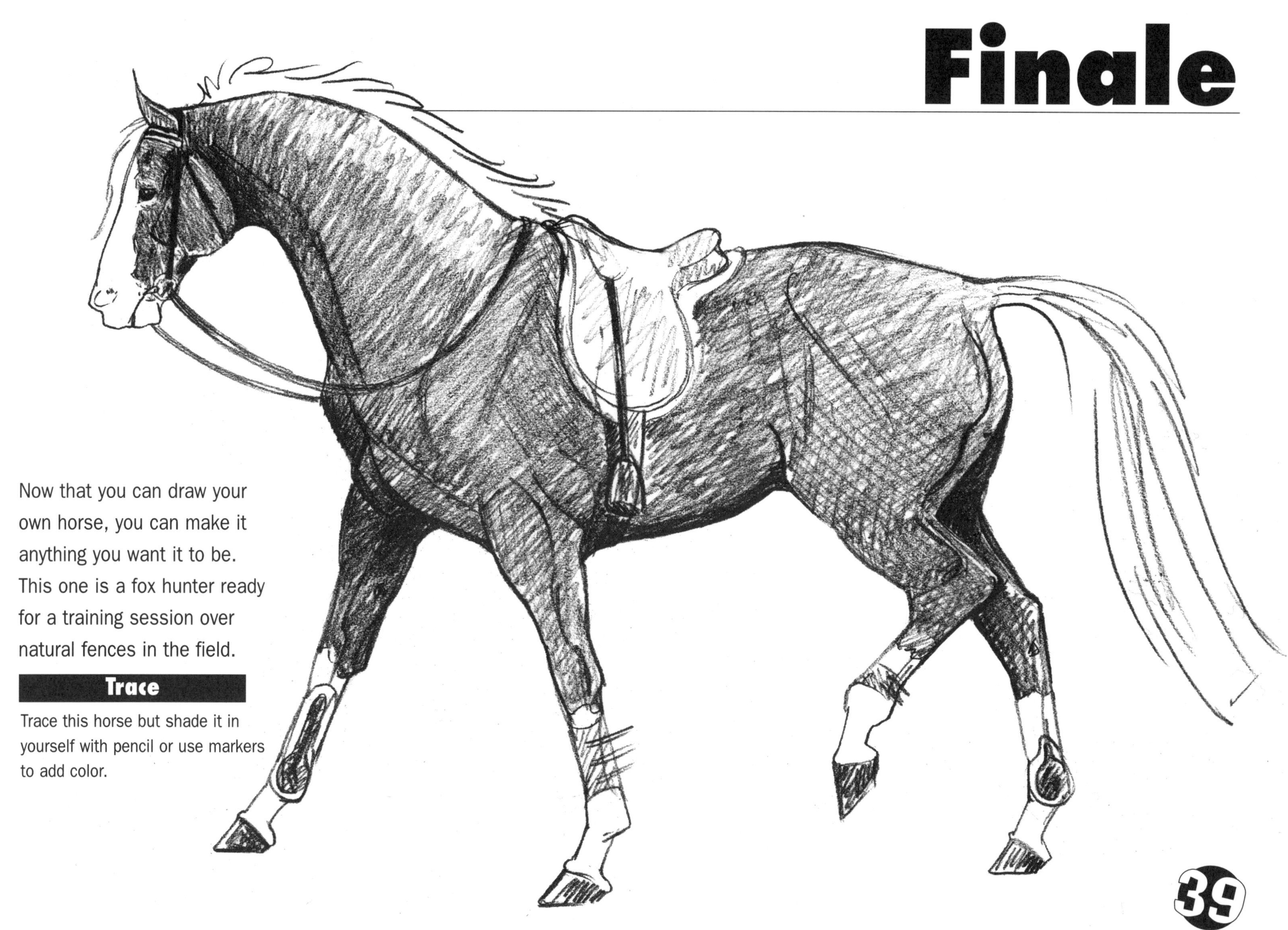

Now that you can draw your own horse, you can make it anything you want it to be. This one is a fox hunter ready for a training session over natural fences in the field.

Trace

Trace this horse but shade it in yourself with pencil or use markers to add color.

Write Us!

- ***Look for other Horse Hollow Press books*** at your local tack store: *The Original Book of Horse Treats* (a cookbook of horse treats), *The Ultimate Guide to Pampering Your Horse* (a guide to handy hints and pampering tips), *The Incredible Little Book of 10,001 Names for Horses* (a listing of thousands of names) and *Trickonometry: The Secrets of Teaching Your Horse Tricks* (all the secrets of trick-training revealed).
- ***Be included in our books:*** Do you have any recipes, grooming tips or handy hints, home remedies, or just comments you'd like to share? Drop us a note; we might use it in an upcoming book!
- ***Send along funny pictures*** of your horse that we can use in upcoming books.
- ***Want to drop a note to the author?*** Send it to June V. Evers at the address below.
- **Write for our free catalog** of products and books for horse lovers.

HORSE HOLLOW PRESS, Inc.
P.O. Box 456, Goshen, NY 10924-0456
www.horsehollowpress.com
e-mail: info@horsehollowpress.com

To order more copies, photocopy this page and mail it to the address below. Or visit your favorite tack & feed store!

Yes! I want to order more books. Please send me:

QTY:

____ *Anyone Can Draw Horses.* $7.95

____ *Trickonometry: The Secrets of Teaching Your Horse Tricks.* $23.95
All the secrets to successful trick training revealed.

____ *The Original Book of Horse Treats.* $19.95
Cookbook of treats and things you can make at home for your horse.

____ *The Ultimate Guide to Pampering Your Horse.* $24.95
Hundreds of pampering tips and handy hints to please your horse.

____ *The Incredible Little Book of 10,001 Names for Horses.* $8.95
Thousands of names for horses and ponies.

____ *Horse Lover's Birthday Book.* $4.95 • A book of days to remember as well as a guide to gifts for horses and humans you can make yourself.

Add $4.95 for shipping & handling per order. Pay only one price for shipping no matter how many books you order.

Total enclosed: $________ (Check, money order, or credit cards accepted. NY residents, please add sales tax.)

OR CALL TOLL-FREE: 1-800-4-1-HORSE to order!

Mail to: HORSE HOLLOW PRESS
P.O. Box 456
Goshen, NY 10924-0456

Name: ______________________________

Address: ______________________________

City/State/Zip: ______________________________

Phone: ______________________________

Visa/MC/AMEX: ______________________ Exp. Date: __________

Signature: ______________________________